The Rat Pack Quiz Book

This is a TV Tidbits book. Other TV Tidbits books include:

The ABC Movie of the Week Companion by Michael Karol
Barnabas & Company: The Cast of the TV Series Dark Shadows by Craig Hamrick
The Classic Television Quiz Book, by Craig Hamrick
The Comic DNA of Lucille Ball by Michael Karol
The Lucille Ball Quiz Book by Michael Karol
Sitcom Queens: Divas of the Small Screen by Michael Karol
The TV Tidbits Classic Television Trivia Quiz Book by Craig Hamrick

The Rat Pack Quiz Book

Includes TV Tidbits & Trivia!

Diane F. Tarlin

Edited by Craig Hamrick & Michael Karol

iUniverse, Inc.

New York Lincoln Shanghai

The Rat Pack Quiz Book
Includes TV Tidbits & Trivia!

iUniverse books may be ordered through booksellers or by contacting:

iUniverse
2021 Pine Lake Road, Suite 100
Lincoln, NE 68512
www.iuniverse.com
1-800-Authors (1-800-288-4677)

Front and back cover designed by Michael Karol ©2006

ISBN-13: 978-0-595-40616-6 (pbk)
ISBN-13: 978-0-595-84983-3 (ebk)
ISBN-10: 0-595-40616-5 (pbk)
ISBN-10: 0-595-84983-0 (ebk)

Printed in the United States of America

To my husband, who encourages me in everything I do.
Thanks for all your support.
Also, to my brother, who urged me to write this book. Enjoy!

"Do not go where the
path may lead, go instead
where there is no path
and leave a trail."
　　—Ralph Waldo Emerson

Contents

Acknowledgements

I'd like to thank Craig Hamrick and Michael Karol for their contributions to this TV Tidbits book. Many thanks also for all the editing they did and sharing with me their knowledge of publishing. You guys are a gas. Thanks!!

List of Contributors

This book features TV Tidbits by Craig Hamrick and Michael Karol: See www.tvtidbits.com for more fun TV trivia.

Introduction

New Jersey, 1960
Small suburban town thirty-five minutes from the Big Apple
Nightfall

Conversation coming from bedroom between author and her sister:
Me: Dean is much cuter!
Her: Not on your life! Jerry makes me swoon!
Me: Dean's voice is dreamy!
Her: Jerry is funnier than Dean!

And on and on it went until I got old enough to leave home and go to college. My sister's passion for Jerry Lewis eventually cooled, but my love of Dean Martin only got stronger through the years. I amassed a large collection of Dean memorabilia, records and tapes. His family was Hollywood royalty and Dean and Jeanne were the first "super-couple" (at least to me!). When Nick Tosches' brilliant bestseller, *Dino: Living High in the Dirty Business of Dreams*, came out in 1992 I was thrilled to finally get an insight into what made this marvelous entertainer tick.

My brother has been a lifelong fan of Lucille Ball. He has written several books on Lucy and suggested that I write one on Dean Martin. Thinking about it, I decided to write about The Rat Pack, which I reasoned might attract a larger audience. Dean is my real passion, but the Rat Pack was awesome and left a large impact on our country in the Swinging Sixties. Indeed, as you'll discover, they are still influencing us today.

This book was written with love and admiration for the five guys who brought so much fun into our lives. They made Vegas the only place to be and if you were lucky enough to catch their act, you were in for a real treat; it was something you would never forget. They captured our hearts and souls and we are still looking for a way to recreate those carefree days in which they ruled. They were the most talented entertainers of their time. Long live the Rats!

Find out how much you know about the fabulous five in the following pages. And have fun.

Diane Tarlin
Boston
Summer 2006

The Frank Sinatra Quiz

1. Where and when was Frank Sinatra born?

2. What were the circumstances of Frank's birth?
a. His mother used a midwife.
b. He wasn't breathing when he was born.
c. His father wasn't present.
d. He weighed less than four pounds.

3. What happened during Frank's birth that would keep him out of the Army?

4. Who had the most influence over Frank?
a. His mother, Dolly
b. His father, Marty
c. His grandmother
d. His Aunt Mary

5. Frank's father, Marty, was a bantamweight boxer, a firefighter and a barkeeper.
What was his bar called?
a. Sinatra's Place
b. Cheers
c. Marty O'Brien's
d. Marty O'Harrah's

6. Who influenced Frank in his obsession for cleanliness?
a. his mother, Dolly
b. his father, Marty
c. his girlfriend, Nancy
d. bandleader, Harry James

> **Frank Fact:** Because of $65 his parents gave him, Frank was able to buy a portable public address system and sheet music arrangements. He started collecting musical arrangements that the bands needed. Not many people could afford this equipment or the arrangements but Frank had them. Many of the bands wanted the arrangements and thus had to use Frank as their vocalist.

7. Frank was an only child and his parents made a comfortable living. Because of this Frank was: (Hint: There is more than one correct answer.)
a. soft spoken, sensitive, sweet
b. impeccably dressed
c. often bullied and beaten up
d. always the class leader

8. The Three Flashes was the first group that Frank sang with. Put these next four groups or bands in the order Frank sang with them:
a. Tommy Dorsey Band
b. Benny Goodman Band
c. Harry James and his Music Makers
d. The Hoboken Four

9. While touring with Harry James, Frank married his hometown sweetheart, Nancy Barbato. They had three children together. What were their names?

10. As a teenager, who would Frank say was his first "singing idol?"
a. Perry Como
b. Ella Fitzgerald
c. Billy Holiday
d. Bing Crosby

11. What was Frank's favorite color? (His house in Palm Springs was decorated in this color.)
a. red
b. blue
c. orange
d. green

12. Frank called this musician his "mentor." He would learn timing and phrasing from him. Who was he?
a. Sammy Cahn
b. Benny Goodman
c. Tommy Dorsey
d. Bing Crosby

13. Harry James wanted to change Frank's name in 1939. What did he want to call Frank?
a. Frankie Trent
b. Frankie Sands
c. Frankie Satin
d. Frank N. Stein

14. What was Frank's first big musical hit, charting in May 1940?
a. "I'll Never Smile Again"
b. "All or Nothing at All"
c. "Stardust"
d. "You'll Never Know"

15. The girls who worshipped Frank in the 1940's were known as Bobbysoxers, because of the socks they wore. What else were they called?
a. Frankaholics
b. Sinatratics
c. Frankatics
d. Swoonatras

16. After divorcing Nancy, Frank was married three more times. Name the Sinatra wives.

17. In January 1942 Frank was named top band vocalist by *Billboard*. He replaced which performer, who also had been #1 on the *Downbeat* popularity poll for six years?
a. Al Jolson
b. Bing Crosby
c. Perry Como
d. Dick Haynes

> **Frank Fact:** On March 7, 1946, Frank Sinatra won a special Oscar at the Academy Awards for his critically acclaimed film on religious and racial intolerance called *The House I Live In*. Frank himself starred in this 10-minute film, took no salary and donated all the profits to anti-juvenile delinquency and drug programs.

18. In the forties, as Frank was becoming more well-known, he often went to Toot Shor's Saloon with this famous comedian. They both enjoyed their Jack Daniel's whiskey. Who was this classic comic?
a. Jack Benny
b. George Burns
c. Jackie Gleason
d. Milton Berle

19. Frank won a Best Supporting Oscar in 1953 for his role in which of the following movies?
a. *The Man with the Golden Arm*
b. *From Here to Eternity*
c. *Pal Joey*
d. *The Manchurian Candidate*

20. Which of Frank's wives helped him get the role in this Oscar-winning movie (as mentioned in question #19)?

> **TV Tidbit:** Frank's TV debut was on *The Bob Hope Special*, a variety special on May 27, 1950. Also on the show was Peggy Lee.

21. Who was the musical director for *The Frank Sinatra Timex Show,* which was televised on October 19, 1959? Frank often praised this man as "the greatest arranger in the world."
a. Sammy Cahn
b. Jimmy Van Heusen
c. Nelson Riddle
d. Ken Lane

22. Who was the lucky actress to receive Frank's first on-screen kiss?

a. Anne Jeffreys
b. Lana Turner
c. Florence Henderson
d. Kim Novak

> **TV Tidbit:** Frank tried two TV series of his own, one in 1952 and one in 1957. Neither became a hit. In 1957 he signed a three million dollar, three-year deal with ABC for 36 half-hour shows. The network was hoping that Frank could boost its ratings. Frank, who did not like rehearsing, taped 11 shows in 13 days. The show was not a hit, and was dropped after 26 weeks.

23. Frank appeared in nearly 60 movies throughout his career. Match these movies to the character Frank plays in them.

Frankie Machine	*The Tender Trap*
Joey Evans	*The Man With The Golden Arm*
Vince Talmadge	*The Manchurian Candidate*
Nathan Detroit	*Pal Joey*
Tony Rome	*The Joker Is Wild*
Charlie Y. Reader	*A Hole In The Head*
Dave Hirsh	*Guys & Dolls*
Danny Ocean	*Come Blow Your Horn*
Pvt. Angelo Maggio	*Some Came Running*
Tony Manetta	*Tony Rome*
Alan Baker	*Ocean's 11*
Joe E. Lewis	*Cast A Giant Shadow*
Capt./Maj. Bennett Marco	*From Here to Eternity*

24. In 1955 Frank feuded with the popular TV show host of *Toast of the Town*. Frank took out an ad in the TV trade papers, addressed directly to this person and called him "sick, sick, sick." Who was this very popular host?
a. Ed McMahon
b. Milton Berle
c. Ed Sullivan
d. Jack Parr

25. In a 1955 Producers Showcase TV musical production of *Our Town*, Frank was the Stage Manager (who narrates the show), with Eva Marie Saint as Emily Webb and Paul Newman as George Gibbs. Newman was not the original choice for George. Which "rebellious" star was the original choice for George?

26. In *Our Town,* Frank sang one of his biggest hit songs. It won an Emmy and would later become one of his signature songs. Years later, it was also the theme song for the very popular TV sitcom *Married With Children..* What was the name of this song?

27. Who wrote the lyrics to Frank's other signature song, "My Way?"
a. Frankie Avalon
b. Bobbie Darin
c. Paul Anka
d. Wayne Newton

TV Tidbit: *TV Guide's* reporters often write about pilot series that are planned. Some are made and some are not. Here are two scripts that were considered for Frank: From *TV Guide* August 6, 1955: "Frank Sinatra and NBC are more than half-serious about a proposed half-hour weekly dramatic show in which Sinatra would play himself, in his own home town." From *TV Guide*, November 12, 1955: "Frank Sinatra is mulling a TV series, *International House*, in which he is cast as the proprietor of a European hotel. It's a whodunit." Neither of these was made.

---

28. What is the song that Frank recorded the most often and that he also disliked the most?
a. "My Way"
b. "Put Your Dreams Away"
c. "Come Fly With Me"
d. "Strangers In The Night"

29. Frank had a hit song from his movie *A Hole In The Head* which he re-recorded to use during the 1960 presidential campaign for John F. Kennedy. The song showcased JFK as the new president for the country. What was the name of this song?

30. In 1965 Frank and Dean Martin made an unannounced appearance on *The Tonight Show*. Who was the host of the show that night?
a. Joan Rivers
b. Johnny Carson
c. Joey Bishop
d. Totie Fields

Frank Fact: From *The Wall Street Journal*, Friday, March 8, 2005: Twin Palms, the Palm Springs home of Frank Sinatra, was sold again for the second time in 10 months. The 1947 home sold to interior designer Barclay Butera, for 2.6 million dollars. Mr. Butera plans to use this house as his main residence after restoring and updating it. The 4,500 square foot house was originally designed for Frank and his first wife, Nancy, by architect Stewart Williams. The home is situated near homes formerly owned by Al Jolson, Jack Benny, and Cary Grant.

---

31. Frank and Sammy Davis Jr. made an appearance on a popular children's TV show, where the host was know for his pie-throwing escapades. Name the host.
a. Pinky Lee
b. Soupy Sales
c. Captain Kangaroo
d. Winky Dink

32. What record label did Frank form in the early '60s?
a. Capitol
b. Apple
c. Reprise
d. Decca
e. Orange

33. On November 16, 1965 Frank was the subject of a one-hour CBS documentary called *Sinatra: An American Original.* Which famous TV personality hosted it?
a. Jack Parr
b. Johnny Carson
c. Walter Cronkite
d. Mike Wallace

34. Frank and Dick Van Dyke co-hosted the twentieth Emmy Awards in 1968. One of the highlights was Frank, Carol Burnett, and Lucille Ball singing "I Remember It Well." Frank opened the show singing a song from *Guys & Dolls*. What was this song?
a. "My Funny Valentine"
b. "Luck Be a Lady Tonight"
c. "There's a Small Hotel"
d. "I Could Write a Book"

TV Tidbit: Though Frank was enough of a television presence to warrant a Hollywood Walk of Fame star for TV, when he was nominated for an Emmy in 1957, as Best Male Singer—at the height of his fame—he lost to Perry Como (the other nominees were Eddie Fisher, Gordon MacRae, and Harry Belafonte).

---

35. In 1973 Frank ended his two-and-a-half year retirement with an album and a TV special. What was the name of this famous TV special?

36. Frank went on entertaining for 25 more years after his comeback. In 1980 he returned to motion pictures after a ten-year absence. He appeared in the movie *The First Deadly Sin*, his last starring role. Who was his co-star in this movie?
a. Angie Dickinson
b. Faye Dunaway
c. Jill St. John
d. Rin-Tin-Tin

37. Frank wanted to play the role of the alcoholic lawyer in *The Verdict*. Who did this role ultimately go to? (Hint: This actor is known for his blue eyes, just like Frank.)

38. Barbara Sinatra's golf buddy was a popular singer and entertainer that Frank was friendly with and enjoyed working with. Eventually he ended up "just putting up with her?" Who was she and why was Frank unhappy with her?
a. Rosemary Clooney
b. Judy Garland
c. Keeley Smith
d. Dinah Shore

39. In 1992 CBS and Tina Sinatra collaborated to bring to TV a four-hour miniseries entitled *Sinatra*. Tina wanted to set the record straight about many of the public misconceptions of Frank. They auditioned about 250 actors for the lead. Who got the role?
a. Harry Connick, Jr.
b. Ray Liotta
c. Phillip Casnoff
d. Frank Sinatra, Jr.

40. In 1993 and 1994 Frank recorded two of his favorite CDs, featuring duets with many other famous singers including Barbra Streisand, Tony Bennett, Liza Minelli, Aretha Franklin, and Steve and Eydie What were these popular CDs titled?

41. On Frank's 80th birthday there was a celebration at the Shrine Auditorium in L.A. What famous rock star, also born in New Jersey, took part in the tribute and said, "On behalf of all of New Jersey, Frank, I want to say, 'Hail, brother, you sang out your soul.'"

TV Tidbit: Frank paid $125,000 to have Elvis Presley on his show on May, 12, 1960.

42. Frank won many awards in his lifetime. How many of each of these did he win?
a. Academy Awards
b. Emmys
c. Golden Globes
d. Grammys

43. How many albums did Frank and Nelson Riddle collaborate on?
a. 6
b. 14
c. 17
d. 21

> **Frank Fact:** Humphrey Bogart once said, "Sinatra's idea of paradise is a place where there are plenty of women and no newspapers. He doesn't know it, but he would be better off the other way around."

44. Name two hobbies that Frank had all his life.
a. Stamp collecting
b. Bowling
c. Painting
d. Golf
e. Train collecting
f. Playing scrabble

45. Which of these awards did Frank win?
a. Congressional Gold Metal of Honor
b. Entertainer of the Century 2000
c. Kennedy Center Honor
d. NAACP Lifetime Achievement Award

> **Frank Fact:** A toast that Frank often made: "May you live to be 100 and may the last voice you hear be mine."

46. Where and when was Frank's last performance?
a. Caesar's Palace in 1995
b. Caesar's Palace in 1996
c. Palm Springs in 1995
d. Palm Desert in 1995

47. What was the last song Frank sang at that performance?
a. "The Best Is Yet To Come"
b. "My Way"
c. "September Song"
d. "Come Fly With Me"

> **Frank Fact:** The heavyweight title fight on March 8, 1971, between Ali and Frazier, took place at Madison Square Garden. Frank took the photograph of this fight that appeared on the cover of *Life Magazine.*

Answers to Frank Sinatra Quiz

1. Frank was born December 12, 1915 in Hoboken, N.J.

2. b. Frank was not breathing when he was born. His grandmother, a midwife, quickly took him and held him under cold water until his lungs drew air and he started to breathe.

3. Frank weighed 13 ½ pounds at birth and his mother was a small woman. The doctor had to use forceps and he pierced one of Frank's eardrums. This would ultimately keep him out of the Army. He also was left with scars on his ear, neck, and cheek. Because of this difficult birth his mother could not have any more children.

4. a. Frank's mother, Dolly. She was a very outgoing, enterprising, and politically conscious woman. She was tenacious and driving. Dolly was a force to be reckoned with and had big ambitions for Frank. She helped him get started in the music business by calling in favors to friends who owned a bar.

5. c. Marty Sinatra's bar was called Marty O'Brien's; that was the name he used as a bantam-weight boxer.

6. a. Frank's mother, Dolly was the big force in influencing Frank's behavior. If Frank wanted something, she was determined that he have it. She was scrupulously clean, and later in life Frank was rumored to shower as much as three times a day, wash his hands constantly and refuse to handle dirty money.

7. a., b., and c. It has been said that as a youngster Frank's personality resembled his father's. He was quiet, thoughtful, and kind. He was always very well dressed and Dolly never let him want for anything. He was often teased about his clothing and about the scarring on his face.

8. d., c., a. and b. The Three Flashes added Frankie to their group and they became The Hoboken Four. In June, 1939 he signed with Harry James and in January, 1940, he left James and went with The Tommy Dorsey Band, a big move up. His first film with the Dorsey Band in 1941 was *Las Vegas Nights*. Frank left The Dorsey Band in September, 1942 and played a few concerts with Benny Goodman at the Paramount Theatre. Benny Goodman was said to be totally shocked when he heard the bobbysoxer's reaction to Frank.

9. Frank's children are: Nancy—born June 8, 1940
Frank Jr.—born January 10, 1944
Christina—born June 20, 1948

> **Frank Fact:** A quote by Harry James at the time: "The kid's name is Sinatra. He considers himself the greatest vocalist in the business. No one ever heard of him. He looks like a wet rag. But he says he's the greatest."

10. c. Billy Holiday. Frank once noted "It was Billie Holiday, whom I first heard in 52nd Street clubs in the early 1930s, who was and still remains the greatest single influence on me."

11. c. Orange. His house in Palm Springs was decorated with so much orange that when he married Barbara Marx in 1976 she hired a decorator to "tone it down" and make it more neutral. Frank said, "Orange is the happiest color."

12. c. Frank would come to think of Tommy Dorsey as his 'mentor' and "almost a father to him."

13. c. Frankie Satin. When Dolly Sinatra heard this she told Frank that "No Sinatra would change his name, he was born a Sinatra, he would stay a Sinatra."

14. a. "I'll Never Smile Again"

15. All the answers are correct. There were many names for these fans of Frank, including Swoonatic, Swoondoggler, Sinatraless, Sinatrabugs, and Sonatra, according to John Lahr in his book *Sinatra: The Man And The Artist*. He wrote, "To the teenagers that screamed for him he was 'Frankie'; to the world he quickly became 'The Voice.'"

16. Nancy Barbato—February 4, 1939-November 1, 1951
Ava Gardner—November 7, 1951-July 5, 1957
Mia Farrow—July 19, 1966-1968
Barbara Marx—July 11, 1976-May 14, 1998 (his death)

17. b. Bing Crosby, who had been one of Frank's idols

18. c. Jackie Gleason

19. b. *From Here to Eternity*

20. Ava Gardner helped Frank get his Oscar-winning role in *From Here To Eternity* by putting pressure on studio boss Harry Cohn and his wife Joan, her friend. Mr. Cohn eventually allowed Frank to read for the part, and he got the role.

21. c. Nelson Riddle was the musical director. Sammy Cahn and Jimmy Van Heusen were the producers.

22. a. Anne Jeffreys. Anne gave Frank his first on-screen kiss in 1944 while filming *Step Lively*. It was during the filming of this movie that Nancy Sinatra gave birth to their second child, Frank Jr. Frank was not present at the birth.

23. They match up like this:
Frankie Machine—*Man with the Golden Arm*
Joey Evans—*Pal Joey*
Vince Talmadge—*Cast a Giant Shadow*
Nathan Detroit—*Guys &Dolls*
Tony Rome—*Tony Rome*
Charlie Y. Reader—*The Tender Trap*
Dave Hirsh—*Some Came Running*
Danny Ocean—*Ocean's 11*
Pvt. Angelo Maggio—*From Here to Eternity*
Tony Manetta—*A Hole In The Head*
Alan Baker—*Come Blow Your Horn*
Joe E. Lewis—*The Joker Is Wild*
Capt./Maj. Bennett Marco—*The Manchurian Candidate*

24. c. Ed Sullivan

25. James Dean was the original choice for George. This prestigious NBC production was the first one to use a new process the network called "living color."

26. The song is "Love and Marriage", written by Sammy Cahn & Jimmy Van Heusen.

27. c. Paul Anka. "My Way" was originally a French Composition with lyrics by Gilles Thibault and Claude Francois Ravaux. Paul Anka, a '50s pop star, composer and lyrist, wrote the English lyrics, and felt Frank would be perfect to record the song. When released in 1969 it never reached #1 but stayed on the charts for 122 weeks.

28. d. "Strangers in the Night," This title song would win four Grammys.

29. The song was "High Hopes", which won an Academy Award. In the movie Frank sang the song with Ron Howard, who played his son.

30. c. Joey Bishop, a charter member of the Rat Pack.

31. b. Soupy Sales. Frank did this as a request from his daughter Tina.

32. c. Reprise. By the late 50's Frank had earned so much money on his Capital contract that he wanted to start his own record label. He proposed a deal with Capitol Records first, but they turned it down, so Frank formed his own label, Reprise.

33. c. Walter Cronkite. A quote from Walter: "People who understand music hear sounds that no one else makes when Sinatra sings."

34. b. "Luck Be a Lady Tonight"

35. *Ol' Blue Eyes Is Back*

36. b. Faye Dunaway

37. Paul Newman got the role.

38. d. Dinah Shore. Frank and Dinah had a good relationship together, recording on radio and television. However, Frank felt that Dinah used her friendship with Barbara Marx to get Barbara to break up with him. He also felt that Dinah was condescending to Sprio Agnew, a good friend of Frank's, when he appeared on her show.

39. c. Phillip Casnoff starred as Frank in the miniseries. He had also starred on Broadway in *Chess* and *Shogun*. Frank reportedly thought the movie was a faithful adaptation of his life, and he and Tina were pleased with Casnoff's performance.

40. *Duets* and *Duets II*

41. Bruce Springsteen

42. Frank won:
3 Oscars
1 Emmy
3 Golden Globes
10 Grammys

43. c. 14 Albums. Frank and Nelson recorded the famous *Strangers in the Night* album in just two days.

44. c., and e. Frank painted for about 50 years, and he hung many of his modern pieces in his Palm Springs home. His other hobby was collecting trains. He had a train room in his Palm Springs home called "All Aboard," which was a replica of his New Jersey hometown, Hoboken. His love for trains started as a child when he would go to New York to see all the train displays in the store windows.

45. Frank won all the awards mentioned. He also won the Grammy Legend Award for Lifetime Achievement in 1994, a Peabody Award in 1965, Jean Hersholt Humanitarian Award from the Academy of Motion Pictures Arts Sciences in 1971 and the Cecil B. DeMille Award from the Hollywood Foreign Press (Golden Globe) in 1970, to name a few. He was also decorated by many foreign countries.

46. c. Frank's last appearance was on February 25, 1995, at the Marriott Desert Spring Resort & Spa for the Frank Sinatra Desert Class Golf Tournament.

47. a. The last song Frank sang was "The Best Is Yet To Come."

Frank Quote: "People often remark that I'm pretty lucky. Luck is only important in so far as getting the chance to sell yourself at the right moment. After that, you've got to have talent and know how to use it."

For Real Frank Lovers: An Expert Quiz

The Chairman of the Board thinks you are a real gas if you can answer these 10 questions in less than one minute.

1. What color were Frank's eyes?

2. What was Frank's favorite color?

3. What was Frank's favorite drink?

4. Name Frank's children.

5. Who was Frank's best friend?

6. In 1957 Frank won the Golden Globe for Best Actor in a musical or comedy, for which film?

7. Which President awarded Frank the Presidential Medal of Honor?

8. In 1966 Frank and his wife were guests on John Daly's *What's My Line*? Who was he married to at the time?

9. In 1988 Frank, Dean and Sammy went on tour. Name it.

10. Where is Frank buried?

Answers to Real Frank Lovers Expert Quiz

1. blue

2. orange

3. Jack Daniels

4. Nancy, Frank, Jr., and Christina (Tina)

5. Jilly Rizzo

6. *Pal Joey*

7. President Ronald Regan, in 1985

8. Mia Farrow

9. Legends Tour, Reunion Tour, or Together Again Tour

10. In Palm Springs, at Cathedral City's Desert Memorial Park

The Dean Martin Quiz

1. Where and when was Dean Martin born?

2. What was Dean's birth name?

3. How many siblings did Dean have?
Extra Credit: What were their names?

4. Dean's Italian father came to America and found a profession in Steubenville, Ohio. What was this profession?
a. worked in the steel mills
b. worked as a croupier
c. worked as a barber
d. worked as a tailor

5. What type of movies influenced Dean?
a. dramas
b. westerns
c. musicals
d. comedies

6. Before Dean made it big, what other jobs did he have?
a. iron worker, drug store worker, shoe salesman
b. butcher, baker, candlestick maker
c. gasoline attendant, shoe-shine boy, croupier
d. newspaper boy, drug-store worker, boxer

7. Dean was beginning to sing at functions in Steubenville when he was suddenly noticed by a band leader who suggested that he change his name. Who was the bandleader?
a. Sammy Watkins
b. Tommy Dorsey
c. Harry James
d. Ernie McKay

8. What was Dean's first stage name?
a. Dino Martin
b. Dino Martini
c. Dean Martini
d. Dean Marshmallow

9. Whose vocal style did Dean emulate?
a. Frank Sinatra
b Bing Crosby
c. Perry Como
d. Al Jolson

10. Lou Perry was Dean's first agent. Dean was broke most of the time, and his wife and children were not living with him. He often bunked with Lou and another singer named Sonny King when staying in New York. What enterprising activity did Dean and Sonny do to make extra money?
a. Performed a comedy and song act in the streets
b. Became singing waiters at a posh New York restaurant
c. Were singing valets as they parked cars
d. Performed boxing matches against each other

11. The funny man of a popular comic team suggested that Dean fix his nose. Who was this comic? Extra credit if you know how much the surgery cost.

12. What was the name of Dean's first wife?
a. Jeanne
b Joanne
c. Elizabeth
d. Kathy

13. How many children did Dean have with his first wife?
a. 2
b. 4
c. 5
d. 6

> **TV Tidbit:** According to the Nielsen Statistics, *The Dean Martin Show* was one of the top 20 shows on television for the years 1966-1970.

14. Dean met his second wife, Jeanne Biegger, in 1948. Where did they meet?
a. in Hollywood at a movie screening
b. at the Orange Bowl Parade in Florida
c. New Years' Eve at a Miami hotel
d. in Las Vegas while Dean was performing with Jerry Lewis

15. Who was best man at Dean's wedding to Jeanne?
a. his son, Craig
b. his manager, Lou Perry
c. his partner, Jerry Lewis
d. his brother, Bill

16. How many children did Dean and Jeanne have?
a. 1
b. 2
c. 3
d. 4

17. Dean, his family, and Jeanne's mother, Peggy, (who lived with them all their married life), rarely took vacations. Every year, however, they always spent Easter at the same place. Name it.
a. Las Vegas
b. Palm Beach
c. Palm Springs
d. Hollywood

18. The Martins lived at what prestigious street address?
a. 1000 Roxbury Avenue
b. 601 Mountain Drive
c. 1000 Bel Air Lane
d. 601 Ocean Drive Boulevard

19. How did Dean and Jerry Lewis meet?
a. They were performing at the same club.
b. They were introduced by Jackie Gleason.
c. They were introduced by Lou Perry, Dean's agent.
d. They were introduced by singer Sonny King.

20. Where did they first meet?
a. New York City
b. The Catskills
c. Hollywood
d. Atlantic City

> **TV Tidbit:** Dean Martin and Jerry Lewis made their television debut on June 20, 1948, on Ed Sullivan's *The Toast of the Town*, which was also the debut of the series itself. It was Dean's only appearance on the show.

21. Dean and Jerry first performed together because of unusual circumstances. What were they?

a. Jerry's agent brought them together to save Jerry's act.

b. Jerry's solo act was taking a dive and the club owner ordered them to work together.

c. Dean needed an opening act for his show.

d. It was arranged by Frank Sinatra, a good friend to both, to save both their careers.

22. Dean and Jerry performed together for the first time in what year?

a. 1945

b. 1946

c. 1947

d. 1949

23. What club did Dean and Jerry first appear in and who was the famous "mob-connected" owner?

24. What prank did Dean and Jerry play in Atlantic City to draw customers to their show?

a. They threw money from their hotel windows.

b. They pretended to drown in the ocean.

c. They rode horses down the boardwalk.

d. They personally ushered anyone from the boardwalk into the theater.

25. Dean and Jerry made 16 movies together from 1949-1956. Put these eight movies in chronological order.

1. *The Caddy*

2. *My Friend Irma*

3. *Hollywood or Bust*

4. *Sailor Beware*

5. *Artists and Models*

6. *My Friend Irma Goes West*

7. *That's My Boy*

8. *Three Ring Circus*

26. Dean's passion was golf. His favorite golf buddies included Fletcher Jones, an L.A. automotive dealer; Bill Ransom, a Beverly Hills realtor; and Bill Bastian, an L.A. meat packer known as the "Corned Beef King." What famous hotel owner's son was also in the group? (Hint: He was at one time married to Elizabeth Taylor.)

27. What was the expression Dean used to describe the type of golf they played?
a. swing and pray
b. whip out golf
c. fore for all
d. pack and play

28. Dean and Jerry appeared as hosts of the *Colgate Comedy Hour* for many seasons. This was a big-budget series of comedy spectaculars on television featuring top name guests. Who was the famous variety show host that this show was competing against on Sunday nights?

29. Who were some of the other famous guest co-hosts on the *Colgate Comedy Hour*?
a. Lucille Ball and Desi Arnaz
b. Fred Astaire and Ginger Rogers
c. Bud Abbott and Lou Costello
d. Bob Hope and Bing Crosby

TV Tidbit: On March 22, 1953 *The Bob Hope Show* had a special episode celebrating the one-hundredth telecast of the *Colgate Comedy Hour* on NBC. Its guests stars were Dean Martin, Jerry Lewis, Bud Abbott, Lou Costello, Eddie Cantor, and Donald O'Connor.

30. Hosting their first *Colgate Comedy Hour* in October 1950, Dean sang which of his famous songs?
a. "Volare"
b. "Return To Me"
c. "Everybody Loves Somebody"
d. "That's Amore"

31. Dean and Jerry performed together for almost 10 years. At what famous nightclub did they perform their last show together?
a. Copacabana
b. Stardust Ballroom
c. Riobamba
d. Rainbow Room

32. Many famous movie, television stars, and comedians were in the audience the night of their last performance. Name three of them.

33. Who was the comedian that climbed on stage and begged them to reconsider their split? (Hint: His nickname was "The Great One.")

34. Dean wore a very distinct cologne manufactured by Faberge.
a. What was the cologne called? (Hint: The first half of its name is also a popular flooring material.)
b. What other famous actor wore this cologne (who climbed Mt. Rushmore in *Northwest by Northwest*)?
c. Why did the company stop making the cologne?
d. Which of Dean's sons also favored the cologne?

TV Tidbit: In 1966 Dean Martin received his only Golden Globe, for Most Popular Television Personality (Male).

---

35. Dean was married for a third time in 1973. Name his wife and their children.

36. After Martin and Lewis broke up, Dean was in debt and desperate. He sold his name to a restaurant and bar on the Sunset Strip.
a. What was the name of this famous restaurant?
b. What television series featured this bar as the next-door neighbor to its fictitious detective offices?

37. Dean made his first solo appearance in 1957 at what Las Vegas hotel?
a. The Flamingo
b. The Desert Inn
c. The Sands
d. The Riviera

38. Ed Simmons, a *Colgate Comedy Hour* writer, helped Dean with his first act in Las Vegas. What did he suggest that Dean do to make his act different so he would stand out from the rest of the pack?

39. MUSIC, MAESTRO—Match these famous Dean Martin songs to the movies he sang them in:

1. "Innamorata"   1. *Bells Are Ringing*
2. "Santa Lucia/Fiddle &
   Guitar Band"   2. *You're Never too Young*
3. "Every Street's a Boulevard
   in Old New York"   3. *Ocean's 11*
4. "That's Amore"   4. *The Silencers*
5. "Ain't that a Kick in the Head"   5. *Living It Up*
6. "Just In Time"   6. *The Caddy*
7. "Everybody Loves Somebody"   7. *My Friend Irma Goes West*

40. After Dean performed his act in Las Vegas, the management signed Dean to a five-year contract. How much money would Dean make per week from this contract?
a. $25,000
b. $50,000
c. $75,000
d. $100,000

A Dean Detail: Irving Berlin, one of Dean's biggest fans, often said that Dean sang "White Christmas" and all of Berlin's songs better than anyone else.

---

41. What was Dean's first solo movie after his split from Jerry Lewis?
a. *Some Came Running*
b. *Airport*
c. *Ten Thousand Bedrooms*
d. *Rio Bravo*

42. What did Harry Cohn, who ran Columbia Pictures, say of Dean's screen test?
a. "He can't act at all."
b. "He can't talk at all."
c. "He doesn't project well."
d. "He isn't good looking enough."

43. Dean had to fight to get a role in this second solo movie, but it was a great success.
a. What was the name of the movie?
b. What actor was originally scheduled to play the role Dean won? (Hint: He later had success as half of *The Odd Couple?)*

44. Dean was paid $250,000 for his role in *Ten Thousand Bedrooms*. He had to take a significant pay cut to be part of the movie in Question 43. What was his salary for this movie?
a. $20,000
b. $25,000
c. $50,000
d. $65,000

45. Dean had a long and illustrious movie career. Match these characters played by Dean to the correct movie they are from:

1. Joe Anthony	1. *Some Came Running*
2. Dee Bishop	2. *Ocean's 11*
3. Jamie Blake	3. *The Silencers*
4. Bill Baker	4. *Jumping Jacks*
5. Steve Laird	5. *Airport*
6. Vernon Demerest	6. *Toys in the Attic*
7. Rick Todd	7. *The Caddy*
8. Chip Allen	8. *My Friend Irma*
9. Matt Helm	9. *Artists and Models*
10. Michael Whitacre	10. *Bandolero*
11. Bama Dillert	11. *4 For Texas*
12. Jeffrey Moss	12. *Cannonball Run*
13. Julian Berniers	13 *The Young Lions*
14. Sam Harmon	14. *That's My Boy*
15. Joe Jarrett	15. *Bells Are Ringing*

46. Which of Dean's famous songs enjoyed a revival in 1987 on the soundtrack of the movie *Moonstruck*?
a. "Everybody Loves Somebody"
b. "Memories Are Made of This"
c. "That's Amore"
d. "Return To Me"

> **A Dean Detail:** During the sixties Dean Martin became the top money-making entertainer in the history of show business. He signed a $34 million contract with NBC, and this, added to his Las Vegas appearances and his record sales, set him apart from all other performers.

47. *The Dean Martin Show* had a successful first season and then ran for nine years on NBC, often landing in the Nielsen top 20. Dean owned Thursday nights at 10:00 pm. What was the very unique aspect of the show that many of the top guest stars complained about?
a. Dean was very difficult to work with.
b. There was not enough rehearsal time.
c. Dean did not participate in the rehearsals.
d. Dean would not socialize with the guest stars.

48. Who were some of Dean's favorite guests that many multiple appearances and often became regulars? (Hint: There is more than one correct answer.)
a. Paul Lynde
b. Dom DeLuise
c. Raquel Welch
d. Bob Newhart
e. Tommy Tune
f. Ann-Margret
g. John Wayne
h. Orson Welles

49. What was the name of the dancer troupe that Dean had on his show every week? They eventually became big stars on Dean's summer replacement show.

a. The Swinging Dolls

b. The Golden Girls

c. The Gold Daughters

d. The Golddiggers

> **TV Tidbit:** Lucille Ball loved Dean Martin, but was not particularly fond of his casual attitude toward rehearsing. They couldn't have been more opposite in their approach to TV: Dean liked to come onstage and wing it, while Lucy was the consummate professional, some would even say overbearing, when it came to rehearsing her later shows, *The Lucy Show,* and *Here's Lucy*. Still, Dean guest-starred on *The Lucy Show* in 1966 (which Ball always said was her favorite episode of the series), and saluted the redhead on the special *CBS Salutes Lucy: The First 25 Years* in 1976, while Lucy performed on his variety show and the *Dean Martin Roasts.*

50. The tenth and final season of *The Dean Martin Show* had a different format. What was this very popular format also used by the Friar's Club?

> **A Dean Detail:** It has been said that Dean Martin conquered more mediums than any other entertainer. He has three stars on the Hollywood Walk of Fame, one each for movie, television, and music. He was one of the wealthiest men in Hollywood, owning land, homes, apartments, and 265,000 shares of NBC, whose parent company was RCA (making him the largest individual shareholder). He also owned a share in the Sands hotel. Dino Crocetti from Steubenville, Ohio had done it all. You can almost hear him saying, "Thanks, Pallie, it was a great ride."

51. Who were some of the stars of this new format?

52. Who was Dean's longtime accompanist, appearing on *The Dean Martin Show*? He also wrote Dean's big hit "Everybody Loves Somebody."
a. Nelson Riddle
b. Sammy Cahn
c. Ken Lane
d. Jimmy Van Heusen

> **TV Tidbit:** In 1985 *TV Guide* published *TV's Greatest Hits*, which told the rankings of the most popular TV shows. It was updated in 1994-1995. Each show was ranked by number of season and audience size. *The Dean Martin Show* ranked #67 out of 100.

53. Dean appeared with his good friend John Wayne in two motion pictures. What were the names of these movies? Can you name any co-stars?

54. How many Emmys did *The Dean Martin Show* receive?
a. None
b. 4
c. 8
d. 10

55. In 1985 a detective comedy/drama TV series entitled *Half Nelson* debuted. It starred a young actor/comedian who played a character named Detective Nelson. Dean played himself in this show as a client and confidant to Detective Nelson. Who was this young actor, who later established himself in such movies as *My Cousin Vinny* and *Goodfellows*?

56. In 1979, what big conglomerate paid Dean several million dollars to be their TV spokesman?
a. Con Edison
b. Phillip Morris
c. American Telephone & Telegraph
d. Alcohol & Tobacco Commission

57. Toward the end of his life, which restaurants did Dean patronize every nite?
a. La Famiglia
b. Beverly Hills Polo Club
c. DaVinci
d. Spago's

TV Tidbit: Reviewing the third year of *The Dean Martin Show*, Jack Gould in *The New York Times*, wrote: "Mr. Martin's gift for likeable self-depreciation is providing an air of spontaneity to supplement his singing style. With Greg Garrison's help he has intuitively found one of the secrets of TV longevity: He doesn't take himself seriously, one of the hallmarks of professionalism."

The Dean Martin Show came about due to an unusual agreement. Dean asked NBC for conditions and a salary that were unheard of at the time. NBC agreed. Dean did not have to rehearse and thus worked only one day a week. Some of his guests were unhappy with this arrangement, but it worked for Dean and made this variety show spontaneous. Over nine years he had outstanding guests, including Bob Hope, Frank Sinatra, Bing Crosby, Jimmy Stewart, Orson Wells, Lucille Ball, Lena Horne, Milton Berle, Sammy Davis Jr., The Mills Brothers, The Andrews Sisters, Muhammad Ali, Debbie Reynolds, Goldie Hawn and Irving Berlin.

In 1999 when Lee Hale's book, *Backstage with the Dean Martin Show* was published, Angie Dickinson said, "There'll never be another Dean Martin. Let's face it, he could do it all—movies, records, night clubs, TV—and he did it spectacularly…*The Martin Show* was the best."

Answers to the Dean Martin Quiz

1. Dean was born in Steubenville, Ohio, on June 7, 1917.

2. Dino Paul Crocetti

3. Dean had one older brother, named Guglielmo, nicknamed William or Bill. He was born in 1914.

4. c. Guy Martin worked as a barber, and owned his own shop. He thought it was important to have a trade and own your own business.

5. b. Dean was deeply influenced by westerns, and his favorite movie star was Tom Mix.

6. Dean held many jobs, but the three he is know for are in answer c.: gasoline attendant, shoe-shine boy, and croupier.

7. d. Ernie McKay noticed Dean and signed him to sing with his band.

8. b. Ernie McKay first changed Dean's name to Dino Martini. He thought people would think that Dino was a cousin of Metropolitan Opera Star, Nino Martini, an extremely popular singer at the time.

9. b. Bing Crosby's vocal style influenced Dean, much as he influenced Frank Sinatra.

10. d. Dean and Sonny often held boxing matches against each other and charged admission.

11. Lou Costello, of Abbott & Costello, suggested that Dean have a nose job. The often-repeated story is that Dean borrowed $500 from at least a dozen people to get the job done. He squandered the money on other things and finally several friends, including Costello and Lou Perry, assembled the money and paid the doctor directly. They obviously felt that this was a good investment, and Dean eventually got the job done. However, in the April 2-8, 1966 *TV Guide*, Dean said that his nose job cost him $600 and he borrowed the money from a bookmaker. Take your choice!

12.c. Elizabeth (Betty) Anne McDonald, whom Dean met in Cleveland, where he was performing.

13. b. Dean and Betty were married from 1941-1949 and had four children.
1. Stephen Craig, born June 29, 1942
2. Claudia, born March 16, 1944
3. Barbara Gail, born April 11, 1945
4. Deana, born August 19, 1948

14. b. Jeanne and Dean met at the Orange Bowl Parade on New Years Eve, 1948. It is said that their eyes met and it was love at first sight.

15. c. His partner, Jerry, was the best man at their wedding on August 26, 1949.

16. c. Dean and Jeanne had three children together.
1. Dean Paul Jr., born November 17, 1951
2. Ricci James, born September 20, 1953
3. Gina Carolyn, born December 20, 1956

17. c. They always spent Easter at their Palm Springs home.

18. b. 601 Mountain Drive, Beverly Hills, CA

19. d. They were introduced by singer Sonny King.

20. a. Dean and Jerry first met in New York City.

21. b. Jerry Lewis was performing in Atlantic City and one of the male singers on the bill took ill. Jerry suggested his "good friend" Dean Martin fill in for him. He told them that he and Dean had a great act together, that the audience would love. The management was getting tired of Jerry's solo act, so they agreed to it. Jerry was told he would be fired if it didn't work. Jerry and Dean very quickly wrote an act, and when they performed it was like magic. The audience loved them together immediately and they only became better with time and practice.

22. b. 1946

23. Dean and Jerry first appeared at the famous 500 Club, owned by Paul "Skinny" D'Amato.

24. b. Jerry would pretend to be drowning in the ocean and Dean would save him. As Dean was giving Jerry mouth-to-mouth recitation, Jerry would suddenly jump up and tell everyone to come see their show at the 500 Club. Then he and Dean would take off running down the beach. After a few shows they did not need to do this anymore. Due to word of mouth, every show was soon filled to capacity.

25.
1. *My Friend Irma*—1949
2. *My Friend Irma Goes West*—1950
3. *That's My Boy*—1951
4. *Sailor Beware*—1952
5. *The Caddy*—1953
6. *Three Ring Circus*—1954
7. *Artists and Models*—1955
8. *Hollywood or Bust*—1956

26. Dean's buddy on the golf course was Nicky Hilton, the eldest son of Conrad N. Hilton. Nicky was director and chairman of the executive committee of Hilton International Co.

27. b. whip out golf. When they finished playing they would "whip out" their money.

28. Ed Sullivan on *The Toast of The Town*

29. c. Bud Abbott and Lou Costello were guest hosts, as were Eddie Cantor, Bob Hope, Jimmy Durante, and Fred Allen.

30. d. "That's Amore"

31. a. The Copacabana

32. Steve Lawrence, Milton Berle, Sammy Davis Jr., and Jackie Gleason

33. Jackie Gleason

34. The cologne was called Woodhue, and it was also worn by Cary Grant. Cary was on the Board of Faberge, and when he died, they stopped making it. Dean's son, Ricci, also liked the cologne.

35. Dean was married to former hairdresser Catherine (Kathy) Mae Hawn on April 25, 1973. It was his last marriage. Dean adopted her young daughter Sacha, and though they got divorced in 1976, Sacha was provided for in Dean's will.

36. The name of the restaurant was Dino's Lodge, and the TV series was the popular *77 Sunset Strip*, starring Efrem Zimbalist Jr., Roger Smith, and Edd Byrnes.

37. c. The Sands

38. Ed Simmons came up with the idea of Dean appearing just a little tipsy, enough to get away with many outrageous things on stage.

39. Dean's songs match up this way:
"Innamorta"/*You're Never Too Young*
"Santa Lucia/Fiddle & Guitar Band"/*My Friend Irma Goes West*
"Every Street's A Boulevard In Old New York"/*Living It Up*
"That's Amore"/*The Caddy*
"Ain't That A Kick in The Head"/*Ocean's 11*
"Just In Time"/*Bells Are Ringing*
"Everybody Loves Somebody"/*The Silencers*

40. a. $25,000, a huge amount of money at the time

41. c. The movie was *Ten Thousand Bedrooms*, and was a huge flop. It also starred Anna Marie Alberghetti, Walter Slezak, Paul Henreid, and Monique Van Vooren.

42. b. He can't talk at all.

43. Dean fought hard to get the part in *The Young Lions*, hoping it would jump-start his career, much as Frank Sinatra did in *From Here To Eternity.* It worked for both of them. Tony Randall was scheduled to play the part that Dean eventually got. *The Young Lions* also starred Marlon Brando and Montgomery Cliff.

44. a. $20,000. Dean took a pay cut of $230,000 from his usual salary to play this role.

45. These are the correct matches:

1 & 7
2 & 10
3 & 12
4 & 14
5 & 8
6 & 5
7 & 9
8 & 4
9 & 3
10 & 13
11 & 1
12 & 15
13 & 6
14 & 2
15 & 11

46. c. "That's Amore" made a huge comeback in 1987, when featured in the movie *Moonstruck* starring Cher, and Nicolas Cage.

47. c. Dean did not participate in rehearsals. He had a stand-in (Lee Hale, who wrote a fascinating book titled *Backstage with the Dean Martin Show*) do his parts. Later, Dean would watch rehearsals on a TV monitor so he would have a good idea of what was going to happen. He felt (as did Frank Sinatra) that rehearsals would weaken his spontaneity. Frequently his guests would complain about this because they were afraid that not rehearsing with Dean would make them look bad.

48. a.,b.,e. Paul Lynde, Dom DeLuise and Tommy Tune were all regulars on *The Dean Martin Show.* Bob Newhart and Ann-Margaret were frequent guests.

49. d. The Golddiggers

50. The Friar's would have a "roast", where they would pay tribute to one person, with all of his/her closest friends being on a dais and "roasting" him/her, telling insults in a loving manner. This proved to be a very popular format.

51. Some of the Dean Martin Roast guests were Johnny Carson, Lucille Ball, Don Rickles, Sammy Davis Jr., Senator Hubert Humphrey, Governor Ronald Regan, Joe Namath, Hank Aaron, Truman Capote, Jackie Gleason, Michael Landon, Bob Hope, Kirk Douglas, Monty Hall, Jimmy Stewart, Betty White, George Burns, Telly Savalas, and, of course, Frank Sinatra.

52. c. Ken Lane appeared with Dean on his weekly show and wrote the smash hit, "Everybody Loves Somebody." This knocked the popular Beatles song "A Hard Day's Night" off the top of the charts, becoming #1 in August 1964.

53. Dean and John Wayne appeared in two westerns: *Rio Bravo* (1959), also starring Ricky Nelson, Angie Dickinson, Walter Brennan, and Claude Akins; and *The Sons of Katie Elder* (1965) which featured Martha Hyer, Earl Holliman, George Kennedy, Dennis Hopper, and Jeremy Slate.

54. a. It may be hard to believe, but *The Dean Martin Show* never won an Emmy.

55. Joe Pesci

56. c. American Telephone & Telegraph (AT&T)

57. Dean ate at La Famiglia restaurant in Beverly Hills nearly every night. When La Famiglia went out business (Dean offered them money to stay in afloat), Dean switched to Da Vinci restaurant. His good friend Mort Viner usually ate with him during the week, and Jeanne dined with him on Saturday nights (even after they were divorced).

TV Tidbit: In July 1956, Dean Martin and Jerry Lewis performed for the last time on TV together. They did a 21-hour muscular dystrophy telethon.

The Dean Martin Show:
A TV Tidbits Quiz

Pallie, how many of these questions can you answer?

1. Name some of Dean's guests on the premier *Dean Martin Show*, which aired September 15, 1965.

2. What gimmick did Dean use to open each show?

3. One of Dean's favorite guests was the understudy for Barbra Streisand in *Funny Girl* on Broadway. Producer Greg Garrison heard of her and booked her for *The Dean Marin Show*. She and Dean clicked immediately. She was a guest many times and credits *The Dean Martin Show* for exposing her talents outside of Broadway. She has recently appeared in the blockbuster movie *My Big Fat Greek Wedding*. Name her.

4. Liberace was a frequent and well-liked guest on the show. What nickname did his friends call him?
a. The Piano Man
b. Libby
c. Ace
d. Lee

5. Name the large singing star who had her own radio show and appeared many times on Dean's show. She often came to rehearsal in her housecoat and with rollers in her hair. She loved Dean and the feeling was mutual. She is well-known for singing a song that stirred the troops in WWII, and became her signature. Who is she? Name the song.

6. On the first *Dean Martin Summer Replacement Show* with the Golddiggers, producer Greg Garrison really wanted a certain Las Vegas comedian to be the emcee. He was not interested. Who was the comedian who replaced him, who later went on to be the center square in *Hollywood Squares?*
a. Jack Carter
b. Dom DeLuise
c. Jan Murray
d. Paul Lynde
e. Shecky Greene
f. Charles Nelson Reilly

7. The Golddiggers became so popular they were asked to play at which Las Vegas Casino without Dean?
a. The Sands
b. The Bellagio
c. Caesars Palace
d. The Riviera

8. Nearly two years before their hit series *Laugh-In* premiered, what comedy team hosted *The Dean Martin Summer Replacement Show?*

9. After the fifth season there was a significant change in Dean's personal life which affected the show greatly. What was this change?

10. In the sixth season of *The Dean Martin Show*, the character of Ken Lane's mother was expanded to a 12-15 minute skit, with the possibilities of a future TV spin-off. First choice for this role was a tall, throaty, theater actress who had just co-starred in *Mame* on Broadway. She starred in *The Golden Girls* on TV. Name her.

Answers to *The Dean Martin Show*: A TV Tidbits Quiz

Answer all 10 questions correctly and you have a reserved space with Dean and the Gang on Thursday nights on *The Dean Martin Show*.

1. Frank Sinatra, Diahann Carroll, Bob Newhart, Jan & Dean, and Joey Heatherton were guests on the first show. There were cameos by Danny Thomas, Eddie Fisher, Steve Allen, and Jack Jones.

2. Dean slid down a fireman's pole.

3. Lainie Kazan

4. d. Lee

5. Kate Smith; "God Bless America"

6. d. Paul Lynde. Shecky Greene was originally offered the job but refused it.

7. d. The Riviera

8. Dan Rowan and Dick Martin

9. Dean and Jeanne got a divorce and he could no longer make "Jeanne jokes." The audience missed hearing about his close family life, and seeing their Christmas family specials, and it showed in the ratings.

10. Bea Arthur

The Sammy Davis Jr. Quiz

1. Where and when was Sammy Davis Jr. born?

2. At what age did Sammy make his stage debut?

3. Who raised Sammy?
a. his mother, Elvira Sanches
b. his father, Sammy Davis, Sr.
c. his uncle, Will Mastin
d. his grandmother, Rosa B. Davis

4. What was Sammy called when he made his stage debut?
a. Silent Sam, the Dancing Midget
b. Short, Shuffling Shoes Sam
c. Silent Sam, the Short Singer
d. Little Sammy with the Singing Feet

5. What age was Sammy when he made his film debut in the musical short *Rufus Jones for President*?
a. 5
b. 7
c. 8
d. 9

6. After he appeared the movie *Rufus Jones for President,* Sammy received tap-dancing lessons courtesy of what great entertainer, about whom he would later recorded a song?
a. Bill "Bojangles" Robinson
b. Mary Tyler Moore
c. Mel "Candy Man" Brooks
d. Ben Vereen

> **Sammy Snippet:** Sammy appeared in another movie after *Rufus Jones for President* with Charlie Chaplin Jr., who was about the same age as him. Charlie's mother, Lita Grey was the star. On the last day of shooting, she told Sammy's father that she felt movies were becoming the new rage, and she wanted to legally adopt Sammy, take him to Hollywood, and make him a star. Sammy's mother and father declined the offer.

7. The act featuring Sammy, his father, and uncle was called:
a. The Amazing Trio
b. Davis, Davis & Mastin
c. The Will Mastin Trio
d. The Davis Duo Plus One

8. In 1941 Sammy was booked into the Michigan Theatre in Detroit to fill in for Tommy Dorsey's regular opening act. Who was the vocalist with the Dorsey Band?
a. Dick Haymes
b. Frank Sinatra
c. Dean Martin
d. Vic Damone

> **Sammy Snippet:** By the time Sammy was 15 he had crossed the United States and Canada 23 times as a touring performer.

9. Sammy joined the U.S. Army and encountered serious racism there. He eventually met a fellow entertainer and songwriter who arranged for Sammy to be transferred to Special Services where for eight months Sammy entertained the troops across the country. This songwriter's father had won the Congressional Metal of Honor for his wartime songs "It's a Grand Ole' Flag", and "Over There". Name this famous songwriter and his son, who share the same name.

10. Sammy had a hot affair with a beautiful blond actress who would later star in Alfred Hitchcock's *Vertigo*. Who was this actress and what happened to their affair?

11. Sammy was married three times. Name his wives and their children.

TV Tidbit: In 1957 Sammy was at the height of his popularity. He was making $25,000 a week at the Sands in Las Vegas and was about to become one of television's first black actors, as the star of a dramatic show for *General Electric Theater*.

---

12. Who gave Sammy his first break on television?
a. Milton Berle
b. Al Jolson
c. Eddie Cantor
d. Lucille Ball

13. How many albums did Sammy record?
a. 30
b. 40
c. 50
d. 58

14. In 1954 Sammy was in a serious car accident as he drove from Las Vegas to Los Angeles. It almost cost him his life. What happened in this accident and what famous pal helped him recover?

15. After his 1954 car accident Sammy's first appearance was at the famous Hollywood club Ciro's. The headliner was Janice Paige. She had written into her contract that the opening act (Sammy) could get no more than two bows. What happened that first night at Ciro's?
a. Sammy completely forgot his lines and his balance was off.
b. Janice Paige had a huge fight with Sammy, and he never opened.
c. Sammy was fabulous and got more than two bows.
d. Frank and Dean appeared on the stage with Sammy, and he was great.

16. On March 22, 1956, Sammy made his Broadway debut in the musical *Mr. Wonderful.* This rags-to-riches story was a vehicle written expressly for Sammy. The show ran for more than 400 performances and launched which big hit song?
a. "Mr. Bojangles"
b. "The Candyman"
c. "Too Close For Comfort"
d. "What Kind of Fool Am I"

Sammy Snippet: About a year after his accident, it was Humphrey Bogart who persuaded Sammy to get rid of his eye patch. Sammy had gotten very comfortable wearing it, and Bogart asked him if he wanted to be remembered "as Sammy Davis Jr.," or "the entertainer with the eye patch?" One night at the Frontier Hotel in Vegas, on the spur of the moment, Sammy took off the patch. The audience was shocked at first, but soon stood up and applauded at this act.

17. Beside Frank Sinatra, name one of the first Hollywood personalities to befriend Sammy and try to help to promote his career?
a. Jerry Lewis
b. Mickey Rooney
c. Tony Curtis
d. Kirk Douglas
e. Ann Southern

> **TV Tidbit**: Television composer Morton Stevens was Sammy's music director from 1950-1960, before moving into TV composing. Stevens is known for the themes from *Hawaii 5-0* and *Policewoman*. He returned as music director for Sammy, Frank, and Dean in the 1980s.

18. In 1966 Sammy got his own weekly variety show. His first guests were the notorious movie stars of the 1963 film *Cleopatra*. Name them.

19. In 1954 while Sammy was playing the Apollo Theatre, he read that a beautiful movie star was in town making the movie "*The Barefoot Contessa*." Sammy called her and asked her to come to the show. She attended, then joined Sammy on stage and posed for publicity pictures with him. The audience was very impressed that she would come to the Apollo. Who was this beautiful movie star, who would later have a great influence on another of the Rat Packers?
a. Lana Turner
b. Marilyn Monroe
c. Ava Gardner
d. Rita Hayworth

20. In 1954 Sammy signed with which recording company?
a. Apollo
b. Capitol
c. Decca
d. Patches

21. After a long film absence, Sammy appeared in the movie *Anna Lucasta* with Eartha Kitt in 1958. He had a part in another classic movie the next year in which he played the character Sportin' Life. Name this movie.

TV Tidbit: Sammy was featured in two television pilots. One in 1969 was called *The Pigeon*, in which Sammy played a private detective working out of Los Angeles. He played Larry Miller and his partner was played by Pat Boone. Executive producers were Danny Thomas and Aaron Spelling. In 1973 he made *Poor Devil*, a comedy, the story of a character named Sammy, a soft touch, bumbling sort of a soul, who tries to redeem himself. This co-starred Jack Klugman, Adam West, and Madlyn Rhue. Neither pilot was picked up.

---

22. In October 1959 CBS produced a lavish 90-minute variety show every other week. On the alternate weeks was *Playhouse 90*. On the first telecast, the guests were Sammy Davis Jr., Rock Hudson, Tallulah Bankhead, Mort Sahl, and Esther Williams. What was this show called?
a. *The Big Show*
b. *The Big Party*
c. *The Big Event*
d. *The Big Surprise*

23. In 1964 Sammy appeared on Broadway in the show *Golden Boy*, for which he earned a Tony nomination. Who was his understudy?
a. Gregory Hines
b. Ben Vereen
d. Mikhail Baryshnikov
d. Johnny Mathis

24. Sammy hosted his own musical/variety show, *The Sammy Davis Jr. Show*, on NBC from January 1966-April 1966. Due to a contract clause, Sammy could do the first show, and then had to have fill-in co-hosts for the next three shows. Which three Hollywood personalities helped Sammy out?
a. Johnny Carson
b. Bob Hope
c. Jerry Lewis
d. Sean Connery

> **TV Tidbit:** Sammy was co-host, with Danny Thomas, of the 1965 Emmy Awards show. Danny Thomas said, "Where else but in America can it happen—an Arab and a Jew on the same show."

25. In 1975 Sammy ventured into the talk/variety show arena. William B. Williams was his co-host and Avery Schreiber was the in-house comedian. The show only lasted for 55 episodes. Why?
a. Sammy was not popular enough to get good guests.
b. Sammy was too energetic to be a host.
c. Sammy and William B. Williams did not get along.
d. His time slot was against Johnny Carson.

26. In 1979 Sammy won a Daytime Emmy nomination for his portrayal of Chip Warren on which soap opera?
a. *All My Children*
b. *General Hospital*
c. *One Life To Live*
d. *The Young & The Restless*

27. Sammy sang the themes for two TV shows starring Robert Blake. Name the shows.

28. Sammy made 6 guest appearances on an unusual sketch TV show that featured stinging social commentary. And, oh, it also featured shapely girls dancing in bikinis covered in body-painted comments. Name the show.

29. Early in his career, Sammy was friendly with a young truck driver who soon became a famous rock'n'roll king. They tried desperately to star in a movie together being made called *The Defiant Ones.* Who was Sammy's rocker friend, and who eventually starred in this movie?

TV Tidbit: In 1990 Dionne Warwick had a TV show titled *Dionne & Friends*. It only lasted 13 episodes. At the end of each show she added a new member to her personal "Walk of Fame." Some of those who were enshrined on this walk were Sammy Davis, Jr., Sarah Vaughn, Ella Fitzgerald, and Martin Luther King Jr.

---

30. Sammy co-hosted the Academy Awards two times. What were those years?
a. 1964 & 1968
b. 1970 & 1975
c. 1972 & 1975
d. 1975 & 1977

31. Bill Cosby's popular TV sitcom, *The Cosby Show,* aired on NBC from 1984 to 1992. Bill recruited famous musicians he loved, to guest star on the show. Name four from the following list.
a. B.B. King
b. Quincy Jones
c. Sammy Davis Jr.
d. Louis Armstrong
e. Lena Horne
f. Dionne Warwick
g. Frank Sinatra
h. Aretha Franklin
i. Stevie Wonder
j. Keely Smith
k. Madonna
l. Luther Vandross

32. In February 1972, what famous TV show, with Sammy as the guest star, won an Emmy for Outstanding Directional Achievement in Comedy? This groundbreaking show had the longest applause for a TV kiss at the time, and caused quite a sensation. Norman Lear directed the show.

33. In 1976 Sammy received the Kennedy Center Honors. Name two of the other honorees that year.

a. Perry Como
b. Irving Berlin
c. Bette Davis
d. Ernest Hemingway
e. Chuck E. Cheese

Sammy Snippet: Sammy Davis, Jr. has been called by many "the greatest entertainer ever." He did it all, vaudeville, radio, television, Broadway, Las Vegas, and motion pictures. He performed comedy, drama, and dance, and excelled at all of them. In addition to having his own TV series, he made numerous appearances on shows, including *General Electric Theater, What's My Line* (three times), *The Lucy Show, Mod Squad, Hullabaloo, The Rifleman, The Steve Allen Show, The Jack Benny Show, The Dick Powell Show, Charlie's Angels, The Flip Wilson Show, The Tonight Show, The Carol Burnett Show, All In The Family, Sanford and Son,* and *The Jeffersons,* to name a few. In 1990, Sammy Davis Jr's 60th Anniversary Celebration won an Emmy for Outstanding Variety, Musical or Comedy special. In 2002 a movie, based on Sammy's life, adapted from his bio *Yes, I Can,* was in the planning stages. Eddie Griffin, a young, hot comedian was set to play Sammy. It has not been made yet.

Answers to the Sammy Davis Jr. Quiz

1. Sammy was born in Harlem, N.Y., on December 8, 1925.

2. Sammy made his debut in vaudeville at the tender age of 3.

3. d. His Grandmother Rosa raised him until his father took him on the road. He called his Grandma "Mama" because he heard his father do the same.

4. a. Silent Sam, the Dancing Midget

5. b. Sammy was 7 years old. He was in the 1933 movie with Ethel Waters.

6. Bill "Bojangles" Robinson. Sammy was surprised at how different his dancing was from Robinson's and most of the other dancers he had seen.

7. c. The Will Mastin Trio, composed of Sammy Davis Sr., Sammy Davis Jr., and his uncle, Will Mastin. The name was later changed to The Will Mastin Trio, featuring Sammy Davis Jr.

8. b. Frank Sinatra was the vocalist with the band. He and Sammy became lifelong friends.

9. George M. Cohan and George M. Cohan Jr.

10. The actress was Kim Novak. Harry Cohn, head of Columbia Pictures had groomed her to become a hugely popular actress, as a back-up for Marilyn Monroe. When he found out about Kim and Sammy, he threatened Sammy that he would have to deal with the mob before he could have Kim. Sammy and Kim broke up, and Sammy quickly married Loray White in 1958, whom he divorced a year later.

11. His wives were:
1. Loray White—1958-1959 (divorced)
2. May Britt—1960-1968 (divorced)
   One daughter Tracey
   Two adopted sons, Mark and Jeffrey
3. Altovise Gore—1970-May 16, 1990 (his death)
   One adopted son, Manny

12. c. Eddie Cantor gave Sammy his first real TV break, on *The Colgate Comedy Hour*. During what was meant to be a one time performance. Eddie used a handkerchief to wipe Sammy's face and then used it on himself. Many viewers were appalled at the contact between a white man and a black man. Hundreds of viewers wrote in and wanted Sammy taken off the show, but Eddie stood firm and invited Sammy back for the rest of the season (three more shows).

13. b. 40 albums

14. Sammy was hit in the face by a pointed object on the steering wheel and lost an eye. He had to wear a patch for months and was very depressed. He did not know if he would ever get his balance back to dance. Frank Sinatra took him to live with him, took care of him, and encouraged him. Sammy's first reappearance on stage was a huge success.

15 c. At Ciro's that night, Sammy pulled out all the stops. He did his great act and impressions of Nat King Cole, Louis Armstrong, Frankie Lane, Mel Torme, and Jerry Lewis. The audience went wild. Sammy and The Will Mastin Trio received eight bows and the management decided that they would be the closing act; Janice Paige would be the opener. They also got their name on the marquis the same size as Miss Paige's, which was unheard of at the time for black entertainers.

16. c. "Too Close For Comfort" was the smash hit from *Mr. Wonderful.* Also starring with Sammy in this show were Chita Rivera and Jack Carter.

17. Mickey Rooney was one of the first Hollywood stars to befriend Sammy. They appeared together on *The Colgate Comedy Hour.* Mickey tried to get him a role in a movie, but Mickey's popularity was waning and he did not have enough clout.

18. Elizabeth Taylor and Richard Burton. The show didn't do well in ratings and was replaced by *Sing Along With Mitch.*

19. c. Ava Gardner graciously accepted his invitation to the Apollo and went on the stage to greet the audience.

20. c. Decca Records. Sammy's debut album was called *Starring Sammy Davis Jr.*

21. *Porgy & Bess.*

22. b. The show was called *The Big Party,* sponsored by Revlon. Although there were supposed to be twenty shows filmed, it was cancelled in December 1959. It never found the right audience.

23. b. Ben Vereen was his understudy. He went on to have a prolific career on Broadway, starring in *Pippin* and *Jesus Christ Superstar*, among other classics.

24. Due to a prior commitment with ABC, Sammy could not appear on the television for three weeks proceeding the special, so Johnny Carson, Jerry Lewis, and Sean Connery filled in for him as guest host.

25. b. It was thought that Sammy's high energy level was too much for the viewers. A good host tends to be calmer, more self assured, not showcase his own skills too often.

26. c. *One Life To Live*—Sammy portrayed Chip Warren in 1979, 1981 & 1983.

27. The shows were *Baretta* (1975) and *Hell Town* (1985).

28. Rowan & Martin's *Laugh-In*

29. Sammy was friendly with Elvis Presley and they both thought this movie was the perfect vehicle for them. Unfortunately Colonel Tom Parker, Elvis's manager, thought the movie was too controversial for Elvis, and while they were trying to work things out, the movie roles went to Tony Curtis and Sidney Poitier.

30. c. Sammy co-hosted the Academy Awards in 1972 and 1975.

31. a., c., e., and i.

32. The show was *All In the Family* with Carroll O'Connor. Sammy kissed O'Connor on the cheek at the end of the show, which surprised O'Connor's character, the bigot Archie Bunker.

33. a. Perry Como, b. Bette Davis and c., Irving Berlin. Also honored were Nathan Milstein and Alwyn Nikolais.

Sammy's Musical Highlights

1. What was the highest position that "Candy Man" reached on the *Billboard* Hot 100?
a. 1
b. 2
c. 3
d. 4

2. "Candy Man" is from the soundtrack of a popular children's film. Name it.
a. *Fitzwilly*
b. *Willy Wonka and the Chocolate Factory*
c. *Flubber*
d. *That Darn Cat*

3. Sammy also had two other top 100 hits in his recording career. The first one was from a Broadway hit called *Stop the World, I Want to Get Off* and asked a musical question. Name the song.
a. "Can I Get A Witness?"
b. "Do You Love Me?"
c. "What Kind of Fool Am I?"
d. "Does Anyone Really Know What Time It Is?"

4. Sammy's third Hot 100 hit came from a Broadway hit called *Golden Rainbow* (1968), which starred Sammy's pals Steve Lawrence and Eydie Gorme. Name it.
a. "I've Gotta Be Me"
b. "Gonna Build A Mountain"
c. "I'm Coming Out"
d. "I'd Like to Teach the World to Sing"

5. The popular song from *Golden Rainbow* made was revived in what 2001 movie starring Tom Greene and Drew Barrymore?

Fill in the words or sentences that are missing in Sammy's hit songs:

6. Who can take a sunrise?
Sprinkle it with dew
Cover it with _____ and a _____ or _____
The Candy Man.

7. If I ruled the world
Everyday would be the first day of _____.

8. That was Mr. Bojangles
Mr. Bojangles
Mr. Bojangles

___ ___ ___ ___.

Answers to Sammy's Musical Highlights

1. a. 1

2. b. *Willie Wonka and the Chocolate Factory*

3. c. "What Kind of Fool Am I" hit number 92 in the top 100 in 1962.

4. a. "I've Got To Be Me" hit number 85 of the top 100 for 1969.

5. *Freddie Got Fingered*

6. Cover it with <u>chocolate</u> and a <u>miracle</u> or <u>two</u>

7. <u>Spring</u>

8. <u>Lord, could he dance.</u>

Sammy Snippet: In 1969 Sammy appeared in Bob Fosse's musical *Sweet Charity*, which some believe is his best movie performance ever.

The Peter Lawford Quiz

1. Where and when was Peter Lawford born?

2. What was Peter's full birth name?

3. What were the circumstances of Peter's birth? (There is more than one answer.)
a. Lady Lawford was 40 years old and almost died.
b. He was three weeks late and weighed nine pounds.
c. He was born eight weeks early and weighed only four and a half pounds.
d. His umbilical cord was wrapped around his neck.

4. What kind of a mother was Lady Lawford?
a. loving, kind and sympathetic
b. caring, but hardly ever around
c. overbearing, interfering, and dictatorial
d. mentally unable to care for the child

5. Peter got his first acting role in English film called *Old Bill*. How old was he?
a. 5
b. 7
c. 9
d. 10

6. Peter did not have any formal schooling. He was taught by governesses and often had tutors who traveled with the family. How did this lack of formal education affect Peter? (There is more than one correct answer.)

a. He learned so much traveling around the world, it did not affect him.

b. He had a hard time making friends because he moved so much.

c. He became charming and worldly to compensate for his lack of education.

d. He was insecure his whole life because of his lack of formal education.

7. By the time Peter was 15 he had traveled around the world how many times?

a. 2

b. 3

c. 5

d. 7

> **Peter's Pearls:** As his cousin Valentine Lawford has said, "Peter wasn't brought up, he was dragged up." According to author James Spada, who wrote *Peter Lawford: The Man Who Kept The Secrets*, during his adolescence, Peter traveled to Australia, Bermuda, Brazil, Ceylon, Cuba, Hawaii, Monte Carlo, Spain, Portugal, Tahiti, the United States, and many more countries. It was then he fell in love with Hawaii, and often returned there.

8. When Peter was 13 he had a serious accident that affected him the rest of his life. What happened?

a. He fell off a tree, broke his leg and it never healed properly.

b. He broke his wrist playing cricket.

c. He slammed his arm through a glass window.

d. He fell off a horse and strained his neck.

9. The Lawfords did not stay in London and eventually moved to Los Angeles. There Peter got his first part in an American film, in a movie called *Lord Jeff.* It was a supporting role with two very popular child stars. Who were they?
a. Roddy McDowell
b. Freddie Bartholomew
c. Mickey Rooney
d. Robert Blake
e. Judy Garland
f. Elizabeth Taylor
g. Lucille Ball

10. Peter went through a dry spell after *Lord Jeff,* and the Lawfords moved around quite a bit. In 1942 they moved back to Hollywood to give Peter another chance at acting. He quickly got a bit part in *Mrs. Miniver* and then went on to make more movies. Which movie did Peter first get noticed in?
a. *A Yank at Elton*
b. *The White Cliffs of Dover*
c. *Someone to Remember*
d. *Pilot #5*

Peter's Pearls: Peter was thrilled to act alongside the MGM contract players. It was said that Louis B. Mayer's roster contained "more stars than there are in heaven." Under contract at that time were Greta Garbo, John Barrymore, Norma Shearer, Clark Gable, Joan Crawford, Judy Garland, Mickey Rooney, Jean Harlow, Spencer Tracey, and many more stars. Peter even developed a crush on Jane Withers, the child actress who would later play "Josephine the Plumber" in a series of commercials for Comet cleanser.

11. Who was the famous actress who dumped Peter for Gene Krupa in 1944? After this experience Peter's attitude changed; he became selfish, cruel, and heartless in his relationships with women.

a. June Allyson

b. Ava Gardner

c. Mae West

d. Lana Turner

12. Peter appeared in more than 50 movies. Which of these are his movies?

a. *At War With The Army*

b. *Easter Parade*

c. *The Bridge on the River Kwai*

d. *Some Like It Hot*

e. *The Long Hot Summer*

f. *Picture of Dorian Grey*

g. *Never So Few*

h. *In the Heat of the Night*

i. *Sylvia*

j. *Cleopatra*

Peter's Pearls: When Peter started at MGM he was inseparable from actors Van Johnson, Keenan Wynn, and Robert Walker. They all loved the beach, motorcycles and were together constantly. Keenan and his wife, Evie, eventually got divorced and Evie quickly married Van Johnson. The joke going around Hollywood was "Who was going to get custody of Peter?"

13. Peter was married four times. He only had children with his first wife, whose brother became President of the United States. Name Peter's first wife (and any others, if you can) and his children.

14. In what year did Peter become a U.S. citizen and why?
a. 1954
b. 1956
c. 1958
d. 1960

15. Of all his in-laws, with whom did Peter get along best?
a. Father-in-law Joseph Kennedy
b. Brother-in-law Robert Kennedy
c. Sister-in-law Jackie Kennedy
d. Sister-in-law Joan Kennedy

> **TV Tidbit:** A frequent and popular guest on the game show *Password*, in 1961 Peter became the all-time champion at the "lightning round," helping his partner get 10 out of 10 correct guesses in only 16 seconds.

16. In 1954 Peter starred in his first television series, which ran for 39 episodes and was well received. He played the part of an ex-college professor who writes a column for the lovelorn. What was the name of the show?
What actor was originally slated to play the lead? (He would eventually go on to have several TV shows under his own name and played Mark Halliday in the Hitchcock classic *Dial M For Murder.*)
a. Ray Milland
b. Robert Cummings
c. Robert Newhart
d. Raymond Burr

17. In 1957 Peter starred in another TV sitcom, this one called *The Thin Man.*

a. Who played the main roles in the original movie of *The Thin Man?*

b. What author created the character of *The Thin Man* in a series of popular books?

c. Who was Peter's TV co-star and what were their character names on the show?

d. What was the dog's name in the movie series and on the show?

e. Who played Lieutenant Harry Evans, NYPD?

(Hint: He won a Supporting Actor Oscar for the 1968 film, *The Subject Was Roses.*)

18. Peter and wife Pat bought a huge mansion in Santa Monica, on the beach. Which head of a major studio had owned the house before him? Peter had interacted with this "giant" before.

a. Louis B. Mayer

b. Hal Wallis

c. Jack Warner

d. Harry Cohn

TV Tidbit: Peter was on *The Ford Television Theater*, a CBS dramatic anthology series, on April 30, 1953. He starred in an episode called *The Son-In-Law.* Some stars who appeared on this series were Vince Edwards, Tab Hunter, Donna Reed, Ernest Borgnine, Judy Holliday, Robert Young, Barbara Hale and Roger Smith. This series launched many impressive careers.

19. In 1958 Albert "Cubby" Broccoli was set to produce a series of five movies based on Ian Fleming's *James Bond* spy novels. Peter was asked to be James Bond. Why did he turn down the offer, and what then relatively unknown actor eventually played James Bond to perfection?

20. Peter had several other names given him by the press. Which two of these was he called?
a. The forgotten Rat Packer
b. Peter Law/Kennedy
c. Peter Packer
d. The brother-in-Lawford
e. Law-in-ford

21. Milton Ebbins played a large part in Peter's life. Who was he?
a. Peter's manager
b. Peter's best friend from London
c. Peter's driver
d. Peter's public relations man

TV Tidbit: Did you know that Peter's son, Christopher Lawford, who looks a lot like his dad, played the role of Philip "Charlie" Brent on the soap opera *All My Children* from 1992-1997? He also had a brief stint on *General Hospital* a few years later.

---

22. Peter and his son Christopher formed a production company to produce their own films. What was this company called?
a. Lawford & Sons Production, Ltd.
b. P & C Production Company
c. Chrislaw Productions
d. Barebottom Productions

23. Peter was very good friends with Marilyn Monroe and had set her up with John F. Kennedy. Marilyn died on August 5, 1960. What was Peter's involvement in her death?

a. He was there when she died.

b. He was the last one to speak to her on the phone.

c. He tried to cover up some of the evidence so the Kennedys would not be implicated.

d. He had no involvement whatsoever.

Peter's Pearls: Despite injuring his arm as a child, Peter was an excellent athlete. He was an accomplished tennis player, and excelled at all beach sports. In 1959 he shot a hole in one while playing golf with Frank Sinatra at Tamarisk, in Palm Springs.

---

24. In October 1955 a TV pilot was made with Peter Lawford and Nancy Gates playing newlyweds. The pilot was aired as an episode of *Screen Director's Playhouse.* What was the name of this pilot, which coincidentally was the name of a famous cartoon duo?

a. Bugs and Bunny

b. Tom and Jerry

c. Minnie and Mickey

d. Donald and Ducks

25. In 1960 a pilot was produced by the William Morris Agency and written by Carl Reiner. Reiner starred as Rob Petrie, a writer for the *Alan Sturdy TV Variety Show,* and Barbara Britton was his wife, Laura. The pilot was financed by Joseph Kennedy and Peter Lawford. It was not picked up. Sheldon Leonard produced a new pilot from a new script by Carl Reiner. What was the name of this new show, and who were its stars?

26. Chrislaw Productions produced a sitcom in 1963 about a pair of identical twins. The star of this show would later win an Academy Award for her portrayal as *Helen Keller.* Who was this '60s actress, whose son starred in *The Lord of the Rings* trilogy?

a. Sally Field
b. Patty Duke
c. Jacqueline Smith
d. Kate Jackson

TV Tidbit: On the Hollywood Walk of Fame, Peter received his star for his contribution to television, although he had appeared in more than 50 movies.

---

27. In the early '70s Peter appeared in a sitcom in which he played the romantic interest of the lead actress. This home-spun, all-American-pie girl is well-known for her films with Rock Hudson in the '60s. Who is this leading lady?

a. Lee Remick
b. Natalie Wood
c. Doris Day
d. Madonna

28. Peter was a popular guest on many game shows. Which of the following shows did Peter *not* appear on?

a. *What's My Line*
b. *You Don't Say*
c. *$10,000 Pyramid*
d. *$20,000 Pyramid*
e. *The Gong Show*
f. *The Match Game*
g. *I've Got a Secret*

29. In a 1971 TV series, Peter played a mystery writer, who was rather absent-minded and always sought the help of his father, an inspector with the New York Police Department. He often came up with the solutions in the most obscure manner. Name the show.

a. *Columbo*
b. *77 Sunset Strip*
c. *Adventures of Ellery Queen*
d. *Felony Squad*

30. Who played Peter's father, the Inspector, in the above series? (Hint: He would go on to become very famous as beloved Colonel Sherman T. Potter in the series *M*A*S*H*.)*

31. What was Peter's final film?
a. *Buona Sera, Mrs. Campbell*
b. *Salt and Pepper*
c. *Body and Soul*
d. *Where is Parsifal?*

32. What was the cause of Peter's death?

33. Who scattered his ashes and where?

Answers to the Peter Lawford Quiz

1. Peter was born in London on September 7, 1923.

2. Peter Sidney Ernest Aylen Lawford

3. a., d. Lady May Lawford was almost 40 years old and the birth was excruciatingly painful. Peter weighed 9 ½ pounds, and the umbilical cord was wrapped around his neck. The doctor struggled getting the baby out. He was pale, listless, and struggling when he was born. A nurse stayed with Peter all through the night and he survived.

Peter's Pearls: May's husband, Ernest Aylen, was not present during Peter's birth because he knew the baby was not his. May had been having an affair with his commanding officer, Lieutenant General Sir Sidney Lawford. May hoped this baby would result in her marrying Sidney, and it did, but they paid a large price for it. When the scandal broke they had to leave London. They were ostracized from their friends, Sir Sidney had to retire, and their son was branded a bastard. They got married and immediately moved to France. However, May got what she wanted: She was to be called Lady Lawford for the rest of her life.

---

4. c. Lady Lawford was admittedly not a good mother. She called Peter "an awful accident." She did not care for infants and he had a succession of governesses and tutors. It was their job to mold Peter into the perfect little boy, teaching him good manners, etiquette, and proper diction.

5. b. Peter was 7 when he starred in *Old Bill.*

6. c., d. This lack of formal education caused Peter to feel inadequate and insecure all his life. He moved around a lot, often did not have playmates his own age and was in the company of adults. Because of his traveling he did have a great knowledge of many different cultures, and he could speak French, Spanish, and German. He could compensate by being charming and worldly. But this couldn't make up for his lack of reading and math skills.

7. b. Peter had traveled around the world three times by the age of 15.

8. c. Peter slammed his arm through a glass window, sliced his upper arm, slit some muscles and tendons, and severed an artery. At first amputation was advised, but May found a doctor who very carefully (and painfully), gave Peter 37 small stitches to the layers of muscle, tendon, and skin. He had severed all the nerves in his arm. He worked hard to make his right arm functional, but was always embarrassed by its deformity.

> **Mommie Dearest:** Lady Lawford had her own set of rules for Peter: what kind of foods he could eat (organic), his health regiment, and how he dressed. She had wanted a baby girl, and Peter was often dressed in pink clothing. Peter's relationship with his mother would progress from bad to worse. Lady Lawford was mettlesome, dictatorial, overbearing and interfering . Peter would end up being the breadwinner of the family. Sadly, Peter, for all his charm and good looks, could never please his mother.

9. b., c. Freddie Bartholomew and Mickey Rooney were the stars of *Lord Jeff*. Peter and Mickey became life-long friends.

10. d. *Pilot* #5. This movie starred Franchot Tone, Gene Kelly, Marsha Hunt and Van Johnson, with Peter hired as an extra. George Sidney directed it and Peter was to play an emotional scene at the end of the movie. George shot Peter's face in a close up, with an airplane flying off to certain disaster. George's wife, Lillian Burns, who was the head dramatic coach at MGM, saw Peter's face and the emotion it registered in that one final dramatic shot, and at her recommendation he was signed to a contact at MGM on June 7, 1943.

11. d. Peter had an eight-month affair with Lana Turner, at which point she dropped him rather casually. She didn't pick him up one morning for work and Peter could not reach her for days afterward. When he did, she said it was over and she was with Gene Krupa.

12. b., f., g., and i. were movies in which Peter appeared.

13. 1. Patricia Kennedy, April 1954-February 1966 (sister of John F. Kennedy)
2. Mary Rowan, October 1971-1975 (daughter of *Laugh-In's* Dan Rowan).
3. Debra Gould, 1976-1977
4. Patricia Seaton, July 1984-December 24, 1984 (his death)

Peter had four children with his first wife, Patricia Kennedy Lawford:
1. Christopher Kennedy Lawford, born on March 29, 1955
2. Sydney Maleia Lawford, born on August 25, 1956
3. Victoria Francis Lawford, born on November 4, 1958
(Her middle name is after Francis Albert Sinatra.)
4. Robin Elizabeth Lawford, born on July 2, 1961

14. d. Peter became a U.S. citizen in 1960 so he could vote for his brother-in-law John F. Kennedy, who was running for President that year.

15. c. Peter and Jackie Kennedy got along famously all his life because they both felt like outsiders in the Kennedy family.

16. The series was called *Dear Phoebe* and also starred Marcia Henderson. It did well in the ratings despite stiff competition from CBS's *Our Miss Brooks* and ABC's *Boston Blackie*. Peter projected star quality in this sitcom, but after a major dispute with one of the show's investors, Alex Gottlieb, Peter decided to end the show after one season. The star originally slated for the show was Robert Cummings.

17. a. The original *Thin Man* movies starred Myrna Loy and William Powell.
b. The book was written by Dashiell Hammett.
c. The TV show featured Peter Lawford and Phyllis Kirk as Nick and Nora Charles.
d. Their dog was named Asta.
e. Oscar-winner Jack Albertson played Lt. Harry Evans. Nina Talbot was also in the cast. Peter owned 25 percent of *The Thin Man.*

18. a. Louis B. Mayer, whom Peter had met in his teens, when he was under contract at MGM studios.

19. Peter turned down the offer to play James Bond because it was a five-film deal at $25,000 per film. At the time he was getting $75,000 per film. The part went to suave, handsome Sean Connery.

20. a., d.

21. a. Milton (Milt) Ebbins was Peter's manager and remained Peter's closest friend and confidant for 32 years. Milt had been road manager for Count Basie's band and then personal manager for Basie and others. Peter met Ebbins and asked Ebbins if he could help him. Ebbins agreed but thought the arrangement would be short-lived. He ended up staying with Peter and being a very loyal friend.

22. c. Chrislaw Productions

23. b. Peter's involvement in the death of Marilyn Monroe has been gossiped about for years. According to the most widely accepted version of events, Peter was the last person she spoke to on the telephone.

24. b. *Tom and Jerry*. Peter and Nancy played Tom and Jerry Macey. Also in the cast were Frank Fay, Marie Windsor, and Charles Lane. The pilot never got picked up.

25. This show eventually became *The Dick Van Dyke Show*, starring Dick Van Dyke, Mary Tyler Moore, Rose Marie, and Morey Amsterdam. The original pilot financed by Kennedy and Lawford was called *Head of the House*.

26. b. Patty Duke starred in *The Patty Duke Show*. Her son, Sean Astin, appeared in *Lord of the Rings Trilogy* as Sam Gamgee.

27. c. Doris Day. Peter played Dr. Peter Lawrence. The show was called *The Doris Day Show*. Other cast members included Larry Storch, Denver Pyle, McLean Stevenson, Rose Marie, Kaye Ballard, and Jackie Joseph.

28. b. *You Don't Say*. Peter also appeared on *Password*.

29. c. *The Adventures of Ellery Queen*. Starring with Peter were E.G. Marshall, Stephanie Powers and Skye Aubrey.

30. Harry Morgan, who was in *M*A*S*H* from 1975-1993, played Inspector Queen.

31. d. *Where is Parsifal?*, in 1983 was Peter's final movie. The movie cast major stars who had not had any box office success for a while, such as Orson Welles and Tony Curtis. The film was a flop and closed after four days of release.

32. Peter died on December 24, 1984, at Cedars-Sinai Medical Center in L.A. His liver and kidneys were failing from a lifetime of overindulgence in alcohol and drugs. He had spent time at the Betty Ford Clinic trying to recover, but he never could erase all the demons that seemed to chase him throughout his life.

33. Peter was cremated and his last wife, Patricia Seaton, scattered Peter's ashes into the Pacific Ocean.

Peter Lawford's Relationship Quiz

To whom was Peter related, and what was their relationship? See if you can pick out the eight people in this list who were part of Peter's family.

1. Maria Shriver

2. John F. Kennedy

3. Lee Raziwill

4. Andrew Cuomo

5. Dick Martin

6. Dan Rowan

7. Caroline Kennedy

8. Maria Callas

9. Robert F. Kennedy

10. Patricia Seaton

11. Victoria Lawford

12. Francis S. Lawford

13. Pamela Harrison

Answers to Peter Lawford Relationship Quiz

The correct answers are:

1. Maria Shriver is Peter's niece by marriage. She is the daughter of Peter's first wife Patricia's sister Eunice Shriver.

2. John F. Kennedy was Peter's brother-in-law. Peter was married to John's sister Patricia.

4. Andrew Cuomo is married to Robert F. Kennedy's daughter Mary, who is Peter's niece by marriage.

6. Dan Rowan was Peter's father-in-law. Peter was married to his daughter Deborah.

7. Carolyn Kennedy was Peter's niece by marriage. She is the daughter of Peter's first wife Patricia's brother, John F. Kennedy.

9. Robert F. Kennedy was Peter's brother-in-law.

10. Patricia Seaton was Peter's last wife.

11.Victoria Lawford is Peter's daughter.

The Joey Bishop Quiz

1. Where and when was Joey Bishop born?

2. What was his birth name?

3. How many siblings did Joey have, and where was he in the birth order?

4. When Joey was 3 months old the family moved to South Philadelphia where Joey's father opened a :
a. launderette
b. coffee shop
c. bicycle shop
d. bakery

5. What other famous actors or performers came from South Philly? See if you can name at least four.
a. Paul Anka
b. Bobby Darrin
c. Mario Lanza
d. Charlton Heston
e. Jack Klugman
f. Tony Randall
g. Eddie Fisher
h. Fabian
i. Bob Hope
j. Bobby Rydell
k. Bobby Vincent
l. Al Martini
m. Frankie Avalon

Bishop's Best: According to Michael Seth Starr in his book *Mouse in the Rat Pack*, when Joey's good friend Buddy Hackett heard how much he weighed when he was born (2 lbs., 14 oz.), he asked, "Did you live?"

6. In 1938 Joey formed a group with three other aspiring show business actors. When one dropped out they changed their name to:
a. The Philly Three Cheese
b. The Three J's
c. The Bishop Brothers
d. The Bowery Boys.

7. Who gave this new group its first break? He was a club owner who liked to feature new performers. Jimmy Durante and Frankie Avalon got their first breaks there also.

8. While Joey was in the U.S. Army he took up a sport that he had loved as a kid in Philly? What was it?
a. tennis
b. swimming
c. long distance running
d. boxing

Bishop's Best: On January 14, Joey married Sylvia Ruzga, whom he'd met in Miami Beach. He worked solo in a club in Cleveland called El Dompo (Really!). He was then drafted into the army, where he earned the rank of sergeant, and for the next 3 ½ years he was Director of Recreation.

9. Who asked Joey to open for him in 1954 at the Copa?
a. Frank Sinatra
b. Dean Martin
c. Perry Como
d. Bing Crosby

10. How many children did Joey and Sylvia have?

11. What was the name of the first game show on which Joey was a panelist for CBS?
a. *The Price is Right*
b. *Let's Make a Deal*
c. *Liar's Club*
d. *Keep Talking*

12. Other regular panelists on this show were Audrey Meadows, Elaine May, Paul Winchell, Ilka Chase, Morey Amsterdam, Peggy Cass, and Pat Carroll. Who were the three hosts of the show?
a. The first host was the co-creator and host of *Let's Make A Deal.*
b. The second host portrayed Rob Petrie in his 1959 pilot *Head of the Family*, which became *The Dick Van Dyke Show.*
c. The third host has had an illustrious career in show business and is the creator of the shows *Jeopardy* and *Wheel of Fortune.*

13. Joey had begun to receive rave notices for his work, but his exposure on one talk show would further accelerate his success. Who was the legendary talk show host who banked on Bishop?
a. Sid Caesar
b. Gary Moore
c. Jack Paar
d. Walter Cronkite

14. Who was Joey's idol?
a. Jack Benny
b. George Burns
c. Bob Hope
d. Jack Paar

15. What character did Joey play in *Ocean's 11?*

16. Joey had a cameo in a gangster movie *Pepe* in which he uttered his-then famous catch phrase. What was it?
a. "Ain't that a kick in the head!"
b. "Would you believe…"
c. "Son of a gun!"
d. "Well, I'll be…

> **Bishop's Best**: Frank Sinatra called him "the hub of the big wheel" and preferred Bishop's humor to that of almost every other stand-up comic.

17. What legendary TV star did Joey have a feud with? (Hint: This host ruled CBS on Sunday nights.)
a. Carl Reiner
b. Ed Sullivan
c. Jackie Gleason
d. Lou Costello

18. In 1957 Joey did a pilot episode that aired during the run of a show that already was a hit on TV. Joey's show would be renamed *The Joey Bishop Show.* What was the name of the host show that starred a Lebanese comedian?

19. *The Joey Bishop Show* was on the air from 1961-1965. Which of the following actors were involved with the show? (Six are correct.)

a. Angie Dickinson

b. Ruta Lee

c. Abby Dalton

d. Lainie Kazan

e. Buddy Hackett

f. Marlo Thomas

g. Corbet Monica

h. Joe Besser

i. Warren Berlinger

j. Bill Bixby

Bishop's Best: According to Michael Seth Starr in *Mouse in a Rat Pack*, Jack Benny thought Joey Bishop was one of the funniest comics he had ever seen. In 1958, while Joey was playing The Sands in Las Vegas, Joey was halfway through his act when a man in the audience stood up and complained loudly, "I'm going home. You're too funny—and too young." It was Jack Benny, who was performing down the street. From then on, he would tell the audience to go see Joey, "the funniest young comic in the business."

20. What instrument did Joey often play on the show?

a. piccolo

b flute

c. mandolin

d. harp

21. One of the regulars on *The Joey Bishop Show* was an ex-member of The Three Stooges who had replaced Shemp Howard. On Joey's show he played a mailman and was so popular that he was asked back for more episodes. He also appeared on Joey's next TV show. Who was he?
a. Moe Howard
b. Larry Fine
c. Joe Besser
d. Curly Howard

> **TV Tidbit:** One of the writers on *The Joey Bishop Show* was Garry Marshall, of *Lavern & Shirley* fame. He often credits Joey with giving his career a start.

22. Joey had another chance at a TV show, this time in the late-night arena. His show, again called *The Joey Bishop Show,* debuted on April 17, 1967, against the ever-popular *Tonight Show* with Johnny Carson. Who was Joey's co-host?
a. Ed McMahon
b. Buddy Hackett
c. Arthur Treacher
d. Regis Philbin

23. Who were Joey's guests on the premiere episode of his late-night show? One would be a future President of the United States, another gal was just "Singing in the Rain," one we had to "make room for," and one had "Georgia on his Mind."

> **TV Tidbit:** Some of the guest stars on the second *Joey Bishop Show* included Barbara Stanwyck, Danny Thomas, Henry Silva, Jack Paar, Marjorie Lord, Vic Damon, Zsa Zsa Gabor, Bobby Rydell, Jack Benny, Jack Jones, and Andy Williams. Curiously, none of the Rat Pack ever made an appearance.

24. On *The Joey Bishop Show* the comic relief during the first season was provided by "The Son of a Gun" players. They would appear from behind several doors and kibitz with Joey. Frank and Dean thought this was the best part of the show. One of these players later appeared on *Rowan & Martin's Laugh-In,* where the same concept was used. Name her.

a. Ruth Buzzi
b. Goldie Hawn
c. Judy Carne
d. Joanne Worley

25. What caused the end of *The Joey Bishop Show*?
a. *The Tonight Show* was way ahead in ratings.
b. Joey and his co-host were not getting along.
c. Merv Griffin started his own late show.
d. ABC had a contract dispute with Joey.

TV Tidbit: After his late night show was cancelled, Joey made many appearances on the *Tonight Show* and TV quiz shows, but the best was clearly behind him. He left Hollywood, moved to Florida, and now spends his days golfing and fishing. The "quiet" Rat Packer, as he was often referred to, is the only one left to give us any true recollection of the fabulous '60s, Las Vegas, and the incredible days with Frank, Dean, Sammy, and Peter. We wish Joey would share his memories of them with his fans, but so far, he hasn't.

26. Joey was a frequent guest host for *The Tonight Show* after his own talk show was cancelled. Other frequent guest hosts were Joan Rivers, Bob Newhart, John Davidson, and David Brenner, but Joey had the most appearances. How many times did he guest host *The Tonight Show?*
a. 98
b. 177
c. 189
d. 206

27. Joey was a guest panelist on a quiz/audience participation show in 1969. Some of its hosts were Rod Sterling and Allen Ludden, and its panelists included Betty White, Dick Gautier, Fannie Flagg, Norm Crosby, and Dody Goodman. What was the name of this show, in which contestants were shown unusual looking objects, and the panelists had to give an explanation of their use? The contestant then had to bet on which panelist was telling the truth.
a. *Liar's Club*
b. *Liar, Liar*
c. *To Tell The Truth*
d. *Show and Tell*

TV Tidbit: On Tuesday, August 29, 1967 in a telephone interview with David Janssen, Joey asked him if he had anything to say now that he was a free man and could not be touched by the law (Janssen starred in *The Fugitive*). "Yes," said Janssen, "I killed her, Joey. She talked too much."

28. How many movies did Joey make with Frank Sinatra?
a. 1
b. 2
c. 3
d. 4

29. In 1981 Joey filled in for old pal Mickey Rooney who was doing a Broadway show with Ann Miller. It was a burlesque review and got rave notices. What was the name of this show that revitalized Mickey's and Ann's careers?

30. What happened in September 1999 that changed Joey's life?
a. He fell off a stage and was seriously injured.
b. His wife Sylvia died after a long struggle with cancer.
c. His son Larry had twins and made Larry a grandfather.
d. He won an Emmy for a guest-starring role in *Law & Order*.

Bishop's Best: Joey owns two small boats, which are named *Sonuvagun I* and *Sunuvagun II*. He also became a member of the Coast Guard Auxiliary, several times rescuing boaters stranded off the coast of Marina del Rey.

---

31. What did Joey have to say about the remake of *Ocean's 11?*
a. Son of a gun…it was great.
b. The guys would have respected it.
c. It's a joke.
d. Who are you kidding?

32. Joey was a guest on one fellow Rat Packer's TV shows fourteen times, four as a variety guest and ten on the dais of various roasts. Name the show.

> **Bishop's Best**: In the late '60s Joey received a citation from Pope John XXIII for his work and help with the Boys Town residences throughout Italy.

Answers to the Joey Bishop Quiz

1. Joey Bishop was born in the Bronx, N.Y., on February 3, 1918.

2. His birth name was Joseph Abraham Gottlieb.

3. Joey was the last of five children. The oldest was Clara, then Morris, Harry, Becky, and Joey. Joey weighed 2 lbs. 14 oz. and at the time was the smallest baby ever born at the Fordham Hospital in the Bronx.

4. c. Joey's father was a mechanic by trade, and when they moved to South Philadelphia he opened a bicycle shop, selling and repairing bikes.

5. c., e., g., h., j., l., and m.

6. c. They called themselves the Bishop Brothers, although they were not related.

7. Frank Palumbo gave The Bishop Brothers their first break at his club, Palumbo's. From there they went to the Havana Casino in Buffalo. After much traveling they ended up in Miami Beach where Joey met his wife, Sylvia.

8. d. boxing. Joey was stationed at Fort Sam Houston where the great welterweight champion Fritzie Zivic was. He began training Joey as a welterweight contender.

9. a. Frank Sinatra. Joey also opened for him in 1952 at Bill Miller's Riviera in Fort Lee, NJ.

10. Joey and Sylvia had one son, Larry, born on August 4, 1947.

11. d. *Keep Talking,* a quiz show that involved ad-libbing, at which Joey was lightning quick.

12. a. Monty Hall
b. Carl Reiner
c. Merv Griffin

13. c. Jack Paar saw Joey on *Keep Talking* and admired his low-key sense of humor. He turned Bishop into a household name.

14. a. Jack Benny

15. In *Ocean's 11* Joey played Mushy O'Connors, an ex-boxing champ and one of Danny's army buddies.

16. c. Son of a gun!

17. b. Ed Sullivan. Joey was upset because he felt that if he went on the show there was always the chance that this act would be cut because other acts were running overtime.

18. The show was called *Make Room For Daddy* and starred Danny Thomas and Marjorie Lord as his wife.

19. c., f., g., h., i., j. Abby Dalton, Marlo Thomas, Corbett Monica, Joe Besser, Warren Berlinger and newcomer Bill Bixby were all on the show.

20. c. mandolin.

21. c. Joe Besser, who when he appeared on the first *Joey Bishop Show,* was a big hit.

22. d. Regis Philbin was Joey's co-host. Regis made headlines by actually walking off the set during a live show. Philbin said he did it because he knew the ABC executives were unhappy with his performance. Others have said that it was a publicity stunt to attract more viewers to the show. In his book *TV Facts,* author Cobbet Steinberg listed this as "one of the most memorable moments in TV history." Co-host Regis responded to critics, "It's one thing to lose your own show, but it's another to lose someone else's." He returned to the show a few days later.

23. Joey's first guests were Ronald Reagan, Debbie Reynolds, Danny Thomas, and Ray Charles.

24. d. Joanne Worley

25. c. Merv Griffin was hired by CBS to host his own late evening show. Joey began to lose ratings and stations; ABC let him go even though he had not fulfilled his contract. He was replaced by Dick Cavett, for much less money. Cavett did not do any better in the ratings. Joey's buy-out was rumored to be $1.2 million over 10 years.

26. b. Joey guest-hosted 177 times for Johnny Carson. In 1971 when Joey again hosted *The Tonight Show* for the first time since his own show had been cancelled, his return made big headlines. He insisted however, that he was just a guest host and not looking for a new show.

27. a. *Liar's Club*

28. b. 2, *Ocean's 11* (1960) and *Sergeant's 3* (1962).

29. The show was *Sugar Babies* and Joey filled in for Mickey for four weeks.

30. b. In September 1999 Sylvia Bishop lost her battle against lung cancer. The Bishops had been married for 58 years and Joey was crushed. Joey and his son, Larry, scattered her ashes in the ocean, as she had requested.

31. c. "It's a joke," Joey said. "There will only be one Rat Pack, and the remake will be a cheap imitation." Many Rat Pack fans thought he was right.

32. *The Dean Martin Show*

Bishop's Best: Did you know that Joey Bishop was the emcee at the inauguration of President John F. Kennedy?

Joey Bishop Movie Word Scramble

Son of a Gun…..can you unscramble these six movies that Joey starred in during his career?

1. Eepp

2. Hoyjnn Loco

3. Ssyteb Dginwde

4. Het Pede Isx

5. Adm God Miet

6. Lyvlea Fo Eth Llods

Answers to Joey Bishop Movie Word Scramble

1. *Pepe*

2. *Johnny Cool*

3. *Betsy's Wedding*

4. *The Deep Six*

5. *Mad Dog Time*

6. *Valley of the Dolls*

The Rat Pack Quiz

How cool were they? They had their own language, plenty of "broads", and seemed to need only each other to have fun. They were the Rat Pack. How much do you really know about them? See how many of these quiz questions you can answer.

1. Who were the members of the original Rat Pack?

2. Who gave the Rat Pack their name?

3. What was the full name of the Rat Pack?

4. What was the credo of the Rat Pack?

> **Rat on Frank:** According to J. Randy Taraborelli in his book *Sinatra—Behind the Legend*, the " Packers loved Frank Sinatra's sense of style, his cool 'habits' and his extravagant lifestyle, which is why he was named Pack Master."

5. Who were eight of the 'associate' members of the Rat Pack?
a. William Holden
b. Eddie Fisher
c. Bob Hope
d. Milton Berle
e. Lucille Ball
f. Shirley MacLaine
g. Ava Gardner
h. George Burns
i. Ernie Kovacs
j. Marilyn Monroe
k. President John F. Kennedy
l. Tony Curtis

6. Match these birth dates to Frank, Dean, Sammy, Peter, and Joey:
1. June 7, 1917
2. February 3, 1918
3. December 8, 1925
4. December 12, 1915
5. September 7, 1923

7. After Humphrey Bogart died, who took over the official leadership of the Rat Pack?

8. Who came up with the idea of the film of *Ocean's 11*, and who helped get the project together?
a. Frank and Sammy
b. Frank and Dean
c. Frank and Peter
d. Peter and Sammy

9. Name the five casinos involved in the plot of *Ocean's 11*.

10. Match the Rat Pack member up with his character from *Ocean's 11*.

1. Frank Sinatra   a. Josh Howard
2. Dean Martin   b. Jimmy Foster
3. Sammy Davis, Jr.   c. Mushy O'Connors
4. Peter Lawford   d. Danny Ocean
5. Joey Bishop   e. Sam Harmon

11. Who played Frank's wife in *Ocean's 11?*

12. Who played Peter's step-father-in-law-to-be in the movie? (Hint: He also played the Joker on *Batman.*)

13. Match these nicknames up with the Rat Packers:
a. The Dago
b. Charlie the Seal
c. The Voice
d. Lady MacBeth
e. The Leader
f. The Needler
g. "Smokey"
h. Slacksey O'Brien
i. Pierrot
j. Tummler
k. Drunky
l. The Frown Prince of Comedy

14. How many wives did the Rat Packers have between them?
a. 12
b. 14
c. 15
d. 16

15. How many children did the Rat Packers have between them?

a.16

b. 18

c. 19

d. 20

16. Which Packer's son, in 1979 received a Golden Globe as New Star of the Year for his role in *Players?*

17. In 1979, who secretly arranged for Dean and Jerry Lewis to be reunited on the Labor Day Telethon?

a. Frank Sinatra

b. Joey Bishop

c. Sammy Davis, Jr.

d. Jeanne Martin

18. When the Rat Pack was playing in Las Vegas, what were some of the other names they were called?

a. The Summit

b. The Clan

c. The Magic 5

d. Frank & Friends

19. Who was the father-in-law to actor Tommy Sands?

20. How many movies did Frank and Dean make together? Name them.

21. In 1963 whose son was kidnapped from Harrah's Hotel in Lake Tahoe?

a. Frank

b. Dean

c. Peter

d. Sammy

22. Who was the "female mascot" of the Rat Pack?
a. Lauren Bacall
b. Angie Dickinson
c. Shirley Maclaine
d. Mia Farrow

> **TV Tidbit**: In 1949 Quigley Publications, which published trade magazines such as *Motion Picture Almanac* and *Television Almanac*, started the T.V. Champion Awards, based on polls from the critics. Dean Martin won in 1968 and 1969 for Best Variety Show, and in 1972 for Best Male Vocalist.

23. The Golddiggers became regulars on *The Dean Martin Show* in 1967. Four years later, what was their name changed to?
a. The Burlesque Babes
b. The Deannettes
c. The Ding-a-Ling Sisters
d. The Ding-Dong Sisters

24. In 1960 Frank Sinatra hosted a television show called *Here's to the Ladies.* One of his guests was the wife of a United States President, whom he very much admired. Name her.
a. Jacqueline Kennedy
b. Pat Nixon
c. Nancy Regan
d. Eleanor Roosevelt

25. Who gave 16-year-old Elizabeth Taylor her first adult on-screen kiss?

26. Whose two families got together for a successful Christmas special in December 1967 on TV?
a. Peter and Sammy
b. Joey and Peter
c. Sammy and Frank
d. Dean and Frank

27. In 1966 one of the Rat Packers made an appearance on *The Lucy Show* and played two roles. Lucille Ball has said that this was one of her favorite episodes. Who was this Rat?

28. What two Rat Packers produced the movie *Salt & Pepper*, and its sequel? What Studio produced this movie?

29. Only one Rat Packer ever won an Emmy. Name him.

30. One of the Rat Packers never seemed to make good choices when it came to motion pictures. He turned down a great opportunity to work with Robert Aldrich in *Whatever Happened to Baby Jane?* The role went to Victor Buono, who got a Supporting Actor Oscar nod. Who was this Rat?

TV Tidbit: In 1971 *The Dean Martin Show* presented two new half-hour pilots that did not sell. The first was called *Powder Room* with Jack Cassidy, Joey Heatherton and Elaine Stritch, and the second was *What's Up?*, hosted by Jackie Cooper, and featuring Tom Bosley, and Marion Mercer.

31. The film *4 For Texas* starred Frank, Dean, Anita Ekberg, Ursula Andress and Charles Bronson. What comedy team was added to the cast, and brought much-needed laughter and fun to the film.

a. Abbott and Costello

b. The Marx Brothers

c. The Three Stooges

d. Laurel and Hardy

32. Jerry Lewis is said to have "gotten back" at Dean by putting a character named "Buddy Love" in a hit movie of his in 1963. Buddy Love is a lounge singer who treats women with very little regard, is very cool and laid back, and is somewhat of a heel. Name this movie?

TV Tidbit: In 1964 ABC gave Jerry Lewis his own big variety show. The network spent huge amounts of money converting an old theater for the weekly live broadcast of the show. The show was awful and was dropped after three months. ABC then renamed the show *The Hollywood Palace* and used guest hosts. Dean was the first host, and when he came out he thanked "Jerry for the building this theatre for me." Dean hosted the program several times and impressed NBC, who eventually signed him (he resisted for a while) to do his own variety show on their network. The rest is history, as *The Dean Martin Show* received high ratings and owned Thursday nights at 10:00 for nine years.

---

33. This United States President was paranoid about his television appearance, and tried to use the medium to change his image. His first cameo appearance was on *Rowan & Martin's Laugh-In.* Who was he and what Rat Packer's show did this President appear on?

34. Two of the Rat Packers co-owned an Italian Restaurant in Beverly Hills, called Puccini. Who were they?
a. Frank and Dean
b. Frank and Peter
c. Peter and Sammy
d. Joey and Sammy

35. Frank's daughter Nancy debuted on his television special on November 1, 1967. Together they had a hit record. Name the record.

36. Judy Garland starred in the opening episode of *Ford Star Jubilee* in 1955. She was supposed to do another show in 1957 but walked out over a format dispute. In 1962 she returned to TV on her own variety show and her first guests were:
a. Frank Sinatra and Bob Hope
b. Frank Sinatra and Dean Martin
c. Frank Sinatra and Sammy Davis, Jr.
d. Frank Sinatra and Bing Crosby

37. When Peter Lawford had the idea of *Ocean's 11,* who did he think of for the lead, Danny Ocean?
a. Robert Mitchum
b. Jeff Chandler
c. Cary Grant
d. William Holden

Rat Pack Facts: They were hip…they were the one and only Rat Pack. Some members had longer staying power than others, but for a few glorious years in the '60s they gave the country something it needed…fun. They had fun with each other on the stage and the audience had fun being there. They were the hottest ticket in Vegas. They all had careers in film and television, and some "dabbled" in music. It has been said that Sammy Davis, Jr. was the greatest entertainer of them all, yet Frank Sinatra was voted Entertainer of the Century in 2000. But Dean Martin was the only one to get three stars on the famous Hollywood Walk of Fame, one each for Television, Movies, and Music. We will never see the likes of them again.

Answers to The Rat Pack Quiz

1. The original members were Humphrey Bogart, Lauren Bacall, David Niven and his wife Hjordis, Judy Garland and her then-husband Sid Luft, super-agent "Swifty" Lazar, humorist Nathaniel Benchley, and Frank Sinatra.

2. According to Jonathan Van Meter in his book *The Last Good Time,* Lauren Bacall was in Las Vegas to see Noel Coward. When she arrived at the table everyone was drunk. She said to them, "You all look like a goddamn rat pack," and the name stuck.

3. The Rat Pack was originally called the Holmby Hills Rat Pack because the Bogarts lived in Benedict Canyon in Holmby Hills.

4. Their credo was "Never rat on a rat."

5. b., d., e., f., g., i., k., and l. Eddie Fisher, Milton Berle, Lucille Ball, Shirley MacLaine, Kirk Douglas, Ernie Kovacs, President John F. Kennedy, and Tony Curtis were all auxiliary members.

6. June 7, 1917 was Dean's birth date.
February 3, 1918 was Joey's birth date.
December 8, 1925 was Sammy's birth date.
December 12, 1915 was Frank's birth date.
September 7, 1923 was Peter's birth date.

7. Frank Sinatra became the leader of the Rat Pack after Humphrey Bogart died.

8. c. Peter Lawford bought the rights to the movie with his wife Pat Lawford, and with Frank at the helm, the movie came to fruition.

9. The Riviera, The Sahara, The Flamingo, The Desert Inn and the Sands were the five Las Vegas casinos scheduled to be robbed on New Year's Eve.

10. 1- d
2- e
3- a.
4- b
5- c

11. Angie Dickinson played Danny Ocean's wife, Beatrice.

12. Caesar Romero played Peter's step-father-in-law to be, Duke Santa.

13. Frank: c., d., e., and h.
Dean: a. and k.
Sammy: g. and j.
Peter: b. and i.
Joey: f. and l.

14. c. 15. Frank had four, Dean had three, Sammy had three, Peter had four, and Joey had one.

15. d. 20. Frank had three, Dean had eight (he adopted one in his last marriage), Sammy had four (three with his second wife and one adopted with his last wife), Peter had four and Joey had one.

16. Dean Martin's son Dean Paul Martin (Dino)

17. a. Frank Sinatra arranged for Dean and Jerry to be reunited on TV. It was a complete surprise to both of them but never really changed their post-breakup relationship, or lack thereof.

18. a., and c. The Rat Pack was also called The Summit and The Clan (to which friends of Sammy objected).

19. Frank was the unfriendly father-in-law to Tommy Sands, who married his eldest daughter Nancy. Rumor has it that when they got divorced, Frank made it impossible for Tommy to work again in Hollywood.

20. Frank and Dean made seven movies together. They are:
1. *Ocean's 11*
2. *Sergeant's 3*
3. *4 For Texas*
4. *Robin and the Seven Hoods*
5. *Marriage on the Rocks*
6. *Some Came Running*
7. *Cannonball Run II*

21. Frank's son, Frank Jr. was kidnapped in 1963. Frank called in all his favors and even called Peter Lawford to see if he could get help from his brother-in-law, Bobby Kennedy. The ransom asked for was $240,000. Frank got the help he needed and Frank Jr. was returned safely.

22. c. Shirley Maclaine was the official "mascot." She knew Dean from *Artists and Models* and also starred with him in *How to Save A Marriage.* She co-starred with Frank and Dean in *Some Came Running* and with Frank in *Can-Can.*

23. c. The Ding-a-Ling Sisters

24. d. Frank had Eleanor Roosevelt as his esteemed guest.

25. Peter Lawford gave Elizabeth Taylor her first adult on-screen kiss in the movie *Julia Misbehaves,* a 1948 motion picture also starring Greer Garson, Walter Pidgeon, and Cesar Romero. Elizabeth thought she was in love with Peter, but Peter was wary about starting a romance with Elizabeth because she was only 16. They did, however, become good friends.

26. d. The Sinatra and Martin families had a wonderful Christmas special which garnered high ratings for the network. On the show were Frank, Nancy, Frank Jr., and Tina Sinatra; Dean, Jeanne, Craig, Claudia, Gail, Deana, Dino Jr., Ricci, and Gina Martin. Sammy Davis Jr. was a guest.

27. This Rat was Dean Martin who appeared in the episode "Lucy Dates Dean Martin." In this show Dean sings "Everybody Loves Somebody" and played a dual role: himself, and Dean Martin's stunt double, Eddie Feldman.

28. Chrislaw produced the movie *Salt and Pepper* starring Sammy and Peter. Peter came up with the idea for the movie when someone said to him that he was "salt" and Sammy was "pepper." In the movie they played Christopher Pepper and Charlie Salt. Peter was having a hard time getting work at this stage of his life and co-producing the movie gave him a vehicle to star in.

29. Frank Sinatra won an Emmy on May 22, 1966, for Outstanding Musical Program, *Frank Sinatra: A Man and his Music.*

30. Peter Lawford never seemed to make the right choices. He declined the role because he did not feel it conveyed the right image for a Kennedy-in-law. Some felt he didn't think he could handle the role, it was too much of a dramatic stretch.

31. c. The Three Stooges made a guest appearance in the movie and it has been said that that was the funniest part of the movie. The movie was not a success.

32. The movie was *The Nutty Professor.* It is said that Dean never saw the movie, although many of his Hollywood contemporaries did, just to see if Buddy Love was indeed Jerry's revenge against Dean.

33. President Richard Nixon appeared on *Rowan & Martin's Laugh-In* and also on several of *The Dean Martin Roasts.*

34. b. Frank and Peter co-owned the restaurant.

35. Their hit was "Something Stupid."

36. b. Frank and Dean were Judy's first guests in a smashing show.

37. d. Peter originally had William Holden in mind for the role of Danny Ocean.

Rat Fact: Actor Eli Wallach, of stage and screen training, was the original choice to play Angelo Maggio in *From Here to Eternity.* This role won Frank Sinatra an Academy Award for Best Supporting Actor.

The Rat Pack Movie Quiz

Match Frank, Dean, Sammy, Peter, and Joey to the movies they starred in.

1. Girl Crazy
2. *Murder's Row*
3. *The Naked and the Dead*
4. *A Guide for the Married Man*
5. *The Kissing Bandit*
6. *Porgy & Bess*
7. *Johnny Cool*
8. *Little Woman*
9. *Ada*
10. *Suddenly*
11. *The Tender Trap*
12. *Valley of the Dolls*
13. *Exodus*
14. *What a Way to Go!*
15. *Son of Lassie*
16. *Nightmare in the Sun*
17. *Texas Across the River*
18. *On the Town*
19. *Sweet & Low*
20. *Pepe*
21. *Meet Danny Wilson*
22. *A Man Called Adam*
23. *Buona Sera, Mrs. Campbell*
24. *Kiss Me, Stupid*
25. *Airport*

26. *Betsy's Wedding*
27. *Where is Parsifal?*
28. *Kings Go Forth*
29. *My Friend Irma*
30. *The Cannonball Run*
31. *The Pride and the Passion*
32. *Easter Parade*
33. *Bells Are Ringing*
34. *The First Deadly Sin*

Answers to The Rat Pack Movie Quiz

1. Peter Lawford
2. Dean Martin
3. Joey Bishop
4. Joey Bishop
5. Frank Sinatra
6. Sammy Davis, Jr.
7. Sammy Davis, Jr., Joey Bishop
8. Peter Lawford
9. Dean Martin
10. Frank Sinatra
11. Frank Sinatra
12. Joey Bishop
13. Peter Lawford
14. Dean Martin
15. Peter Lawford
16. Sammy Davis Jr.
17. Dean Martin
18. Frank Sinatra
19. Sammy Davis Jr.
20. Peter Lawford, Joey Bishop, Sammy Davis, Jr.
21. Frank Sinatra
22. Sammy Davis Jr.
23. Peter Lawford
24. Dean Martin
25. Dean Martin
26. Joey Bishop

27. Peter Lawford
28. Frank Sinatra
29. Dean Martin
30. Sammy Davis Jr., Dean Martin
31. Frank Sinatra
32. Peter Lawford
33. Dean Martin
34. Frank Sinatra

Score:
30-34 correct—You're super, pallie!
24-29 correct—Ring-a-ding-ding.
11-23 correct—Quizzes ain't your bag, eh?
0-10 correct—You're nowhere, man.

The "What did you say, Pallie?" Quiz

The Rat Pack had their own language, which they used often to confuse others. See if you can guess the meaning of the following phrases that were some of their favorites.

1. Bird, used as, "How is your bird?"

2. Charley, used as "Hi, Charley."

3. Bag, used as "Singing's my bag."

4. Hey-hey, used as "Did you get any hey-hey?"

5. Ring-a-ding, used as "What a ring-a-ding movie."

6. Nowhere, used as "He's nowhere."

7. Duke, used as "Did you duke him?"

8. Clyde, used as "Pass the clyde."

9. Barn-burner, used as "She's a real barn-burner."

10. Gas, used as "That movie was a gas."

Answers to the "What did you say, Pallie?" Quiz

1. *Bird*—The male or female genitalia: a Rat Pack standard greeting was, "How's your bird?"

2. *Charlie*—A generic term for anyone whose name has been forgotten.

3. *Bag*—A person's interest, job, or hobby.

4. *Hey-Hey*—A little action from the opposite sex.

5. *Ring-a-ding*—A term of approval, as in a ring-a-ding broad. Often used with a second "ding" for emphasis.

6. *Nowhere*—Failure.

7. *Duke*—To tip.

8. *Clyde*—Used frequently for many different things. "Pass the clyde" might mean "pass the salt." "I don't like her clyde" might mean "I don't like her behavior."

9. *Barnburner*—A very classy, hip person.

10. *Gas*—Great, fabulous

Appendix

The 1998 death of Frank Sinatra brought Rat Pack mania to the country again. HBO produced *The Rat Pack* movie, starring Ray Liotta as Frank Sinatra, Joe Montegna as Dean Martin and Don Cheadle as Sammy Davis Jr. At this time there were also rumors of a Martin Scorsese movie on the life of Dean Martin based on the Nick Tosches bio, *Dino: Living High in the Dirty Business of Dreams*. This hasn't happened yet.

What has happened is a real explosion of all things Rat Pack. In 2001 a remake of the classic *Ocean's 11* was made, starring George Clooney (as Danny Ocean), Brad Pitt and Julia Roberts. This smash hit was followed by the equally popular *Ocean's Twelve*, and *Ocean's Thirteen* is in pre-production now, said to be released in 2007. Also in 2003 the movie *Martin & Lewis* was made, with British actor Jeremy Northam playing Dean, and Sean Hays as Jerry Lewis.

Coming to us in print has been a plethora of books on the members of the Rat Pack. Ricci Martin wrote *That's Amore: A Son Remembers Dean Martin* in 2002 and Michael Seth Star wrote *Mouse in the Rat Pack,* also in 2002. Will Haygood wrote *In Black and White: The Life of Sammy Davis, Jr.* in 2003, Deana Martin wrote *Memories Are Made of This* in 2004. And in 2005 came Christopher Lawford's *Symptoms of Withdrawal: A Memoir of Snapshots and Redemption* and Jerry Lewis's *Dean & Me: (A Love Story).* These books all give exceptional insight into the lives of the fabulous Rat Pack members, yet at the same time they still remain as elusive to us as ever.

Today there is a Rat Pack Returns Show and a Frank & Barbra (Streisand) Show playing to thousands of audiences in Las Vegas; on tour is a two man show entitled Mr. Bojangles, the Ultimate Entertainer, which is a live stage show highlighting the musical career of Sammy Davis Jr. Dean Martin's son Ricci is touring with a "Tribute to Dean Martin Show" and Frank is still with us at the London Palladium, with an extravaganza which celebrates his music and life with songs at the peak of his career.

At the present, being built in Long Island City, NY is a Frank Sinatra School of the Arts, a 998 student high school with state of the art classrooms and entertainment centers. This should be completed in 2008. In May 2006 Nancy Sinatra got a star on the Hollywood Walk of Fame. Frank would be proud.

Joey Bishop is the only Rat Packer still alive today. Up to this point he has no desire to share his memories with the public.

Rat Pack mania will be with us forever. The allure of those heady, carefree times in the sixties is something we would all like to recreate, or at least be a part of somehow. By keeping the Rat Pack alive we are part of it…and we love it.

Bibliography

Books

Brooks, Tim and Earle Marsh. *The Complete Directory to Prime Time Network and Cable TV Shows 1946-Present,* New York, Ballantine Books, 1979.

Casleman, Harry and Walter J. Podrazik. *Watching TV—Four Decades of American Television.* New York: McGraw Hill, 1982.

Chintala, John. *Dean Martin A Complete Guide to the "Total Entertainer".* Exeter, PA, Chi Productions, 1998.

Davis, Tracey with Dolores A. Barclay. *Sammy Davis Jr.: My Father.* Los Angeles: General Publishing Group, 1996.

Davis Jr., Sammy, and Jane and Burt Boyar. *Yes I Can.* New York: Farrar, Straus and Giroux, 1965.

Davis Jr., Sammy. *Hollywood in a Suitcase.* NewYork: William Morrow and Co., 1980.

Frew, Tim. *Sinatra.* New York, Barnes and Noble, 1998.

Gehman, Richard. *Sinatra and His Rat Pack.* New York: Belmont, 1961.

Gelman, Morrie and Gene Accas. *The Best in Television—50 Years of Emmys.* New York, General Publishing Group, Inc. 1998.

Hale, Lee and Richard D. Neely. *Backstage with the Dean Martin Show.* Taylor Trade Publishing, 1999.

Harris, Jay S. *TV Guide The First 25 Years,* Triangle Publications, 1978.

Lahr, John. *Sinatra—The Artist and the Man.* New York, Random House, 1997.

Lawford, Patricia Seaton with Ted Schwarz. *The Peter Lawford Story—Life with the Kennedy's, Monroe & the Rat Pack.* New York: Carroll & Graf Publishers, Inc. 1988.

Levy, Shaun. *Rat Pack Confidential.* New York, Doubleday, 1998.

Lewis, Jerry, and James Kaplan. *Dean & Me (A Love Story).*New York, Doubleday, 2005.

Martin, Deana with Wendy Holden. *Memories Are Made of This.* New York: Harmony Books, 2004.

Martin, Ricci with Christopher Smith. *That's Amore, A Son Remembers Dean Martin.* New York, Taylor Trade Publishing, 2002.

Marx, Arthur. *Everybody Loves Somebody Sometime (Especially Himself): The Story of Dean Martin and Jerry Lewis.* New York: Hawthorn, 1973.

McNeil, Alexander M., Total Television. Penguin Books, New York, NY. 1996.

Quirk, Lawrence J. and William Schoell. *The Rat Pack: Neon Nights with the Kings of Cool.* Dallas, TX, Taylor Publishing Company, 1998.

Schoell, William. *Martini Man: The Life of Dean Martin.* Dallas, TX, Taylor Publishing Company, 1999.

Shulman, Arthur and Roger Youman. *How Sweet It Was— Television: A Pictorial Commentary with 1434 Photographs.* Shorecrest Publishing, 1966.

Sinatra, Nancy. *Frank Sinatra, An American Legend.* New York: General Publishing Group, 1995.

Spada, James. *Peter Lawford: The Man Who Kept the Secrets.* New York: Bantam, 1991.

Starr, Michael Seth. *Mouse in the Rat Pack.* New York, Taylor Trade Publishing, 2002.

Steinberg, Cobbett. *TV Facts.* New York, Ballantine Books, 1980.

Sullivan, Robert and Editors of Life,. *Remembering Sinatra: A Life in Pictures.* New York, Life Books, 1998.

Taraborrelli, J. Randy. *Sinatra—Behind the Legend.* Secaucus: Carol Publishing Group, 1997.

Terrace, Vincent, *The Complete Encyclopedia of Television Programs 1947—1976, Volume 1-A-K,* New York, A.S. Barnes & Company, 1976.

Tosches, Nick. *Dino: Living High in the Dirty Business of Dreams*. New York: Dell, 1992.

Weiner, Ed and the editors of *TV Guide*. *The TV Guide TV Book*. New York: Harper Collins.

Wilke, Max, *The Golden Age of Television—Notes from the Survivors*, New York, Delacorte Press, 1976.

Articles

Architectural Digest, December 1998, "Frank Sinatra: Inside the Legendary Performer's Palm Springs Compound", David McClintick.

Life Magazine, August 13, 1951, "Crackpots Hit Jackpot."

Look Magazine, May 17, 1966, "Dean Martin cools it…and makes it…" by Betty Rollin.

Look Magazine, December 26, 1967, "Dean Martin Talks About…", by Oriana Fallaci.

Newsweek, May 25, 1998, "The Kid From Hoboken", by Karen Schoemer; "A Man ad his Cufflinks" by Rick Marin, and "The Final Curtain."

TV Guide, June 5, 1953, "Martin & Lewis Backyard Movies."

TV Guide, Sept 28-Oct.4, 1968, "This Man Earns More Money in a Year Than Anyone in the History of Show Business," by Dick Hobson.

Vanity Fair, May 1997, "When They Were Kings", James Wolcott.

Vanity Fair, April 1999, "The Color of Love", Sam Kashner.

Websites

Big Bands and Big Names: **www.bigbandsandbignames.com**
Dean Martin Fan Club: **www.deanmartinfancenter.com**
The Sinatra Family Site: **sinatrafamily.com/news/news.php**
The Internet Movie Database: **www.imdb.com**
Port Halcyon: Your Portal to the Golden Days of Music, Fashion, Culture, and Lifestyle: **www.porthalcyon.com**
The Official Sammy Davis Jr. Website: **www.sammydavis-jr.com/**
Find Famous People Fast!: **www.who2.com**

978-0-595-40616-6
0-595-40616-5

23934359R00084

Made in the USA
Middletown, DE
08 September 2015